Suddenly, they were there again, flitting in and out of the shadows, running through the rooms, not yelling this time but silent, hurrying, tripping over themselves. The Avenger shrank back from the window. He could not afford to be seen. It was important to remain hidden. To bide his time. To wait.

Wait for what?

To wait for his revenge.

"I am The Avenger," he whispered to the night. "And I will avenge this house and what has happened in it."

He knew he would have to be patient. He would have to find out their names and track them down, one by one. He would have to plan a course of action. But he was expert at that kind of thing, had spent long hours observing, spying, witnessing. He was skilled at making plans and then carrying them out methodically, one step at a time. Like with Vaughn Masterson, knowing the right time and the right place to strike.

By the time the trashers had left the house, the tears on the cheeks of The Avenger were cold and hard, like tiny pieces of glass.

WE
ALL FALL
DOWN

Robert Cormier

To Sam and Rosalie Chillemi
for All the Years of Friendship

Published by
Bantam Doubleday Dell Books for Young Readers
a division of
Bantam Doubleday Dell Publishing Group, Inc.
1540 Broadway
New York, New York 10036

The trademark Laurel-Leaf Library® is registered in the U.S. Patent
and Trademark Office.

The trademark Dell® is registered in the U.S. Patent and Trademark
Office.

ISBN: 0-440-21556-0

RL: 6.3

Reprinted by arrangement with Delacorte Press

Printed in the United States of America

September 1993

10
OPM

WE
ALL FALL
DOWN

PART
ONE

They entered the house at 9:02 p.m. on the evening of April Fools' Day. In the next forty-nine minutes, they shit on the floors and pissed on the walls and trashed their way through the seven-room Cape Cod cottage. They overturned furniture, smashed the picture tubes in three television sets, tore two VCRs from their sockets and crashed them to the floor. They spray-painted the walls orange. They flooded the bathrooms, both upstairs and down, and flushed face towels down the toilet bowls. They broke every mirror in the place and toppled a magnificent hutch to the floor, sending china cups and saucers and plates and assorted crystal through the air. In the second-floor bedrooms, they pulled out dresser drawers, spilled their contents on the floor, yanked clothing from the closets and slashed the mattresses. In the downstairs den, they performed a special job on the spinet, smashing the keys with a hammer, the noise like a crazy soundtrack to the scenes of plunder.

There were four of them and although their vandalism was scattered and spontaneous, they managed to invade every room in the house, damaging everything they touched.

At 9:46 p.m., fourteen-year-old Karen Jerome made the mistake of arriving home early from a friend's house. She was surprised to find the front door ajar and most of the lights on. The sounds of yelling and whooping greeted her as she stepped into the foyer.

One of them, still holding the hammer that had demolished the piano, greeted her.

"Well, hello . . ." he said.

No one had ever looked at her like that before.

At 9:51 p.m., the invaders left the house, abandoning the place as suddenly as they had arrived, slamming the doors, rattling the windows, sending shudders along the walls and ceilings. They left behind twenty-three beer cans, two empty vodka bottles, and damage later estimated at twenty thousand dollars, and, worst of all, Karen Jerome, bruised and broken where she lay sprawled on the cellar floor.

The Avenger watched it all.

From his hiding place.

He watched in horror as they trashed the house he had come to love, ransacking and rampaging, the sound of carnage making him wince as if his own body were being ravaged.

Tears stung his eyes, blurring his vision until he blinked them away. This house was his territory. He had staked it out and claimed it for his own. He had become a part of the place and the Jeromes who lived in it, like a son and brother to them all. He had observed the family's comings and goings, had shared their daily routines, their good times and bad times.

Leaving his hiding place, The Avenger scurried from

window to window, flitting in and out of the shadows, protected by the trees and shrubbery that surrounded the house. But these same trees and shrubs also prevented anyone in the other houses on the street from seeing what was going on inside. What was going on horrified The Avenger. "Animals," he muttered as he watched the trashers running from room to room, screaming and yelling, tearing the place apart.

He did not know their names, had never seen them before, but he knew who they were. They were regular kids, not sleazies from Rock Point or the rough guys and dropouts who hung out at Bryant Bridge. They were nicely dressed. No leather jackets or black boots. They looked like high school baseball players or baggers at the supermarket or clerks at McDonald's.

The Avenger did not see Karen Jerome enter the house but he saw her being dragged across the front hallway. A moment later, the lights went out.

A small moan escaped his mouth, a sound that came from a place deep and dark inside of him because he could not help her. That was the most terrible thing of all, knowing that he could do nothing at this moment. He was outnumbered, unable to charge into the house and rescue her.

So, he waited. He was good at waiting. He closed his eyes and opened them again. The house was still dark. And quiet. Were they gone? Had they slipped out quietly while his eyes were closed?

Suddenly, they were there again, flitting in and out of the shadows, running through the rooms, not yelling this time but silent, hurrying, tripping over themselves. The Avenger shrank back from the window. He could not afford to be seen. It was important to remain hidden. To bide his time. To wait.

Wait for what?

To wait for his revenge.

"I am The Avenger," he whispered to the night. "And I will avenge this house and what has happened in it."

He knew he would have to be patient. He would have to find out their names and track them down, one by one. He would have to plan a course of action. But he was expert at that kind of thing, had spent long hours observing, spying, witnessing. He was skilled at making plans and then carrying them out methodically, one step at a time. Like with Vaughn Masterson, knowing the right time and the right place to strike.

By the time the trashers had left the house, the tears on the cheeks of The Avenger were cold and hard, like tiny pieces of glass.

Jane Jerome was still numb two hours after returning from the hospital where her sister Karen lay in Intensive Care, hooked up to all kinds of machines, beeping sounds like small squeals of anguish. Karen's face and hands were the only parts of her body that had been visible. Her face, like a stranger's face, shrouded in white, seemed to be floating in all that whiteness. Her hands were tiny, helpless, fingers curled slightly inward.

Jane wanted to hold those hands, press them to her cheek, ask her pardon and forgiveness. Earlier on the evening of the assault, she and Karen had argued. The usual stupid argument. Karen was a borrower, took Jane's things all the time without asking permission, used her cologne, wore her blouses and sweaters. All of this was kind of humiliating because Jane was two years older and Karen should have been the small kid sister but there she was, fully developed, Jane's size but more style-conscious, improvising, taking one of Jane's sweaters, blending it with one of her own scarves, and, tra la, a smashing outfit.

Guilt assailed Jane as she scrunched herself into her father's big leather chair in the den, listening to him talk to the detective in the living room. A lot of guilt particularly because Jane had shouted at her: *Will you please go have an accident?* one of the favorite phrases at Burnside High this year. What had happened to Karen was much worse than an accident, of course, worse than being struck by a car. It was savage, brutal, personal. Made the damage to the house seem minor by comparison. Not really minor, though. Both attacks were devastating and she knew that life in this house would never be the same.

Funny. At first, when her father had been transferred from Monument, she had hated this house along with Burnside High, hated leaving her old friends and classmates at Monument High, some of whom she had known since kindergarten. But in the months since, she had made friends at school—Patti Amarelli and Leslie Cairns, in particular—and they had shown her the sights, especially the Mall in downtown Wickburg, with its splashing fountain and stores like Filene's and Brooks, and the wild store on the second level where she bought the posters that covered the walls of her room and the Pizza Palace where the guys and girls gathered to eat and hang out.

The ConCenter was located across from the Mall and all the big stars appeared there—New Kids on the Block and Billy Joel and Madonna—and although she didn't often attend performances, it was neat to be around early in the evening, watching the limos pull up, disgorging people from Boston and Worcester, but most of all knowing that the stars were staying at the Wickburg Hilton around the corner. She had caught glimpses of Billy Joel one night as he emerged from the Hilton and that brief look was more intimate, more *personal* than seeing him onstage from a distance.

All of this meant nothing now. Not with Karen in the hospital, in a coma, and the house in ruins, her mother so stunned and heartbroken that Jane could barely stand to look at her. And her father simmering. That was the word. Not raging mad but simmering, anger swirling around inside of him, building to a boil.

As he spoke now to the detective, her father was barely controlling that anger. Making herself small in the big chair, she listened, hardly daring to breathe.

"Ever since we moved here, almost a year ago, it's been happening. Small stuff, ridiculous in a way but . . ." His voice trailed off, muffled a bit.

"What kind of small stuff?" The detective did not resemble a movie and TV detective. He was short and fat and had a squeaky voice, as if somebody were squeezing his Adam's apple. Two cops in uniform had spent hours here yesterday, and today the detective in regular clothes had shown up.

"Phone rings, nobody on the line. A stone tossed through the window last month. Marie, my wife, planted tomatoes last year and they got all torn up, scattered around the backyard. A dead squirrel in the mailbox."

"You never reported those incidents?"

"No," he said, biting off the word. Jane could picture his face getting red. She knew the symptoms, that tight voice, his words like firecrackers. He was getting ready to blow up, something that happened probably only once a year. But when he finally lost his temper, watch out. Yesterday, he had answered these questions patiently but today he was ready to explode.

"Call the police?" he asked, his voice rising a bit. "About tomato plants, phone calls, a dead squirrel?"

Then the detective asked a new question:

"Do you have any enemies, Mr. Jerome?"

Yipes, her father, enemies. The thought was ludicrous. He was Mister Good Guy. Business manager of the telephone company in Wickburg. Wore white shirts, striped ties, smiled a lot, played golf on Saturday afternoons, went to church with his family on Sundays, served on the United Way committee every year. Who could possibly be his enemy? Although she would never admit it aloud to anyone, her father was a sweetheart. He never gave her a hard time or any grief at all. Never grounded her, never ran out of patience with her or Karen or their younger brother, Artie, who was at the peak of brathood. As a result, Jane tried to do things to please her father, to merit not being grounded.

"Do I have any enemies?" Her father's voice was suddenly like a little kid's voice, uncertain, puzzled.

She had to get out of there, didn't want to listen anymore, hated hearing her father being questioned, hated the way he sounded vulnerable, a little scared. It made her feel vulnerable and scared too.

Out on the back porch, in the freshness of the April morning, she flung herself into the old wicker rocking chair. Ordinarily, she would have fled to her room, where she could always find comfort and consolation. But her room, too, had been ruined. She had loved that room, the predominance of blue, her favorite color. And all her favorite things. Her special glass menagerie of frogs and puppies and kittens. The posters on the wall—New Kids and Bruce and messages like AFTER THE RAIN, THE RAINBOW, so many posters that her father said he could have saved the price of wallpaper if he'd known about her poster madness. The room was her turf, her refuge, her hiding place. Where she could close the door and shut out the world, the C-minus in math—the worst mark of her life—the zits popping out all over her face, the agony of Timmy Kearns ignoring her completely after that first date. Her place of retreat to which she admitted only Patti and Leslie, with standing orders for everyone else to stay out.

Standing at the door in the first moment of discovery, seeing the torn mattress, her precious animals spilled on the floor, the posters hanging in shreds, yellow veins on the wall which she did not immediately recognize as pee, the puddle of vomit on the floor, she had grown weak, watery, felt as if she herself had been assaulted. She wanted to flee Burnside, get out of there, back to safe and sane Monument, deadly dull but peaceful, where her father played golf with the chief of police and everybody knew everybody else, even the names of the dogs and cats. A few minutes later, Karen had been discovered in the cellar, and the anger she had felt in her room paled beside the horror of what had happened to Karen.

"Damn it, damn it," she muttered now, rocking furiously in the chair, filled with anger and guilt and—what? She stopped rocking suddenly, sat still in the chair as she caught a movement down near the hedges, past the cherry tree. Somebody or something moving furtively, a blurred image, not quite seen, and then gone. She shivered, drew her arms around herself, wondering if the trashers might be lurking in the vicinity, had returned to the scene of the crime like they said criminals did.

When Buddy Walker broke the mirror in the girl's bedroom, using the Statue of Liberty, a splinter of glass struck him in the cheek and he saw blood oozing on his face in the mirror's jagged reflection. He stared at it drunkenly, dropping the statue to the floor.

Actually, he did not know whether he was drunk or not. He was dizzy, yes, and giddy, and felt like he was floating, his feet barely touching the floor. The lights hurt his eyes, but otherwise he felt pleasantly willy-nilly, letting himself go, carried along by this terrific feeling of drift, thinking: the hell with everything and everybody. Especially home.

The cut was minor, despite the blood. In the middle of all the carnage, the screaming and the shrieks of laughter and the sounds of destruction from the floor below, he made his way carefully to the bathroom and found a box of Band-Aids in the cabinet above the sink. He removed two of them, slipped one into his shirt pocket for later use and, after wiping away the smear of blood with a towel, calmly applied the other Band-Aid to his cheek. His hand was steady despite a sudden swirl of dizziness. The dizziness was pleasant, in fact, as he maneuvered himself back to the bedroom where he leaned against the doorjamb, scrutinizing the damage: the posters hanging in tatters, the collection of small animals scattered on the rug, the torn blankets and sheets, the yellow stains of piss on the wall.

Suddenly, his earlier exhilaration vanished, replaced by a sense of despair, emptiness. He felt isolated from the others, separate from the howls of jubilation and the sounds of crashing and bashing below. *I'm going to be sick.* He dropped to his knees, almost in slow motion, as vomit rushed up his throat and streamed out of his mouth onto the soft blue carpet. The smell, acid and foul, invaded his nostrils. He retched, once, twice, kneeling in the doorway, retched again and again, until nothing came up. His stomach hurt, his chest hurt, his throat hurt.

He became aware of a sudden silence from downstairs, as if Harry and his stooges were listening to him being sick. Rising to one knee, he began to gather his strength, his arms and legs trembling. He averted his eyes from the puddle of vomit on the floor.

Why so quiet down below?

Pressing his hands against his stomach, he lurched toward the stairs, steadying himself against the wall. He wanted a drink. Was desperate for one, although he did not know how he would manage to swallow the booze with the taste of vomit still like acid in his mouth and throat.

On the landing halfway down the stairs, he spotted a half-full bottle of vodka and giggled. He never giggled when he was sober, so he must be drunk. He placed his hand over his mouth to stifle further giggles and picked up the bottle. Still quiet downstairs. The lights out, too. He took a big swig from the bottle, grimacing as the vodka bombed down his throat, bracing himself for the lurch of sickness in his stomach. Instead, warmth spread throughout his body as if he were bathing in the glow of something beautifully soft and fuzzy.

He heard a sound, a moan. Or a gasp. Not sure which. Cradling the bottle in his hand, he went down the remaining stairs, hesitating in the foyer, squinting, and saw, finally, what was going on in the front hallway.

Harry Flowers had a girl against the wall. She was pinned there by Marty Sanders and Randy Pierce. They were holding her arms to the wall while Harry screwed her. Or was he screwing her? Buddy didn't know if you could screw somebody standing up like that. But he was doing something. His pants and striped shorts were halfway down his legs, his ass gleaming in the light spilling in from the front porch. The girl's face was partly hidden in shadows but he saw her frantic eyes, wide with horror. Randy's right hand was like a suction cup on her breast.

"Jesus," Buddy said, the word exploding from his mouth like the vomit a few minutes ago upstairs.

"Me next," Marty said, grinning at Buddy. He was small and wiry and did not weigh much over one hundred pounds but had this big foghorn voice. "Wait your turn, Buddy."

The girl looked directly at him now, her eyes agonized, pleading, and Buddy drew back into the shadows. He wasn't sick anymore. Wasn't anything. As if he had stumbled out of his own life into another, a new existence altogether. He blinked, hugging the bottle as he would a newborn baby.

"Jesus," he said again, his voice a whisper.

Suddenly, Randy howled with pain, and the girl was loose. One moment pinned to the wall, the next moment, free. Not really free but pulling away from her captors while Randy danced around, holding his hand to his mouth, sucking at it. "She bit me," he cried in disbelief.

"You bitch," Harry yelled as he fell backward, tripping over his pants and shorts, which were now down around his ankles. "Get her," he ordered in a tight, deadly voice.

Nobody moved, not even the girl, as if they were caught in the flash of a camera's naked bulb like a picture on the front page of a newspaper. Then: movement, swift, like fast-forward on a VCR, Randy sucking at his hand, Harry now doing his own dance as he pulled up his pants, Marty grabbing at the girl. The girl tore herself away from Marty's grasp, gathering her torn blouse around her breasts. But she had nowhere to go, really, and ran blindly into the wall while Harry, pants pulled up at last, threw himself toward her, yelling, "Bitch."

Buddy saw that the girl had not run into a wall but against a door. She tried to open the door as Harry grappled toward her. Crazy: she was trying to escape into a closet. When she pulled the door open, he saw that it was not a closet but the doorway to the cellar. As the door swung open, Harry leaped toward her, grabbing at her body, his fingers raking her back. She swiveled to avoid his grasp and the movement gave Harry enough time to fling himself forward. But he did not grab her. Instead, he pushed. With both hands. Pushed at her shoulders, once, twice. The girl screamed as she fell forward down the stairs.

Buddy closed his eyes against the sound of her falling. A long time ago, when he was a little kid, he had been in his father's car when it struck an old man crossing the street. He had never forgotten that sound. Like no other sound in the world. Not like a bat hitting a ball or a hammer hitting a nail or a firecracker exploding or a door slamming. The sound had a hollowness in it and in this hollow place was the smaller sound that had haunted his dreams for weeks. That small sound was the sound of something human being struck. And that was the sound Buddy heard as the girl tumbled down the stairs, a series of terrible bouncings, while Harry managed to pull up his trousers and zipped his fly as if he had just finished peeing in the bathroom.

"Let's go, bloods," he said.

Harry was talking black this week.

Later, in the car, driving from Burnside to Wickburg, Marty and Randy discussed the merits of ketchup and mustard on hamburgers and hot dogs. Marty insisted that ketchup should never be used on hot dogs while Randy said that ketchup could be used on anything because it had an American taste.

"What do you mean—American taste?" Marty asked, disgusted, voice deep, like an old-time radio announcer's.

"I mean ketchup is American. Like the Fourth of July, Thanksgiving. Can you imagine a Frenchman or Italian in Europe using ketchup?"

"How do you know? Have you ever been to Europe?"

The argument went on and on as Buddy stared out the window at nothing in particular. He found it hard to believe that Marty and Randy were engaged in a conversation about ketchup and hamburgers and hot dogs so soon after what had happened back in that house while Harry hummed softly as he drove the car, carefully, slowly. Harry always drove slowly, loved to frustrate drivers behind him, holding his speed down to ridiculous levels, until they tried to pass and then he'd speed up gradually, until the other driver realized he was being baited.

"All right, how about mustard?" Randy said. "Mustard works better on hot dogs. I hate it at McDonald's when I find mustard in the hamburger."

"McDonald's doesn't put mustard in its hamburgers," Marty said. "They put a slice of pickle in the hamburger and ketchup but no mustard."

"Of course they put in mustard," Marty boomed. "Next time you're at McDonald's, look at the hamburger. Lift up the bun and take a look. You'll see the hamburger and the pickle and the ketchup but look real close and you'll see the mustard."

Buddy touched the Band-Aid on his cheek. The cut didn't hurt and was not bleeding anymore. He concentrated on the street, letting the stupid argument in the backseat flow around him. At least it kept him from thinking. Thinking of that house, how he had stood there, doing nothing, while Harry raped a girl. A kid, for crying out loud.

Silence came from the backseat now: argument over, the debate of mustard versus ketchup concluded.

"We relax now, bloods," Harry said suddenly, quietly. "We out of their jurisdiction now. We safe and sound."

Buddy pressed his lips together to keep himself from yelling: stop calling us bloods, for crissakes. Harry's black talk was ridiculous because it was not black at all but Harry's version of black. He liked to pretend he was a street kid, from some mythical inner city instead of the son of a prominent architect. Harry was probably the whitest kid Buddy knew. Blond, wore white painter's pants, white socks, white Nikes.

"You did good, real fine, bloods," Harry said. "Followed orders nice." The only order Harry had given: Don't break any windows. "Nice, nice." Still talking his version of black. Last week, he had affected a British accent after seeing an old movie on cable about British soldiers in India. He had pronounced it "Injia."

No one had mentioned the house and the rape since they fled the place. When they stopped at Jedson Park where they cleaned up at the fountain, Buddy had studied the faces of the others, glancing at them cautiously. Their actions were calm and deliberate as they splashed their faces with water. Marty brushed an invisible spot of dirt from his suede flight jacket. The jacket looked old but was new, three hundred dollars' worth of new. Buddy knew how much the jacket cost because Marty put price tags on everything. Randy's jeans also looked old but were new. We pay a lot of money to make things look old, Buddy thought. Harry Flowers was meticulous as usual. Spotlessly clean. Blond hair so neat that it seemed like a wig. Handsome face unblemished, serene as he washed his hands.

Back in the car, Marty and Randy had begun their ridiculous conversation about hamburgers and hot dogs and then fallen into silence. Nobody in the car seemed to mind the silence except Buddy.

Finally he asked: "Why'd you pick that particular house, Harry?" He had other, more important questions to ask but had to begin somewhere.

"Dumb luck, blood."

Blood again.

"Not dumb, smart," Randy called from the backseat.

Randy Pierce followed Harry around school like a big overgrown pet, an invisible tail wagging every time Harry paid him the least attention. Marty Sanders was a smaller version of Harry Flowers, thin and wiry, trying always to be cool but betrayed by a sharp tongue, the tendency to come up with a wisecrack to fit any situation. The first time he saw Randy and Marty together, Buddy flashed back to an old movie on television: *Abbott and Costello Meet Frankenstein.* Marty was clearly Abbott, the sharp guy, the agitator, while Randy was Costello, the buffoon, overweight, often looking bewildered. Glancing at Harry now as he turned onto North Boulevard, he decided that Harry was Frankenstein, the doctor who created the monster.

Who is the monster then? Buddy wondered. Remembering his part in the vandalism and his inability to stop what they had done to the girl, he thought: Maybe it's me. *But I am not a monster.* Or is that what all the monsters said?

"We shouldn't have left the girl like that," Buddy heard himself saying.

"What did you say?" Harry's voice crackled as he brought the car slowly to a halt under a streetlight, the kind of light that casts a ghastly glow on people's faces. Harry's face was stark and purple as he turned to Buddy.

"Listen carefully, Buddy," he said, all traces of black gone from his voice. "You wanted fun, we had some fun . . ."

"That wasn't fun," Buddy said. "Raping a girl, for crissakes." How he could use a drink, wishing now he had not abandoned that vodka bottle at the girl's house.

"You jealous?" Marty piped up from the backseat.

"She wasn't raped," Harry said. "We didn't have time

to rape her. Didn't even get her nice little white panties off."

"But you pushed her down the stairs," Buddy said, hearing Harry's intake of breath, wondering if he had gone too far.

"Maybe I was trying to grab her and save her from falling," Harry said, his voice suddenly mild and reasonable. "Maybe it only looked like I pushed her. What do they say, Buddy? Looks are deceiving."

Although his voice was mild, it contained an undertone Buddy could not pin down. His eyes were dark and piercing as he looked at Buddy. All of which made Buddy shiver inside, realizing that Harry somehow was giving him a message, telling him what to believe.

"Maybe we weren't even going to rape the poor girl," Harry continued. "Just having a little fun with her. She shouldn't have been there in the first place . . ."

But it was her house, Buddy wanted to say. *We were the ones who shouldn't have been there in the first place.* He didn't say anything, held by Harry's eyes. Hated himself for not saying anything but still said nothing.

"Accidents happen," Harry said, leaning toward Buddy, his breath heavy with stale booze. "Understand, Buddy?"

Buddy nodded, eager to end the conversation, eager for Harry to turn away, eager to get away from him.

"Say you understand, Buddy."

Buddy was conscious of the silence in the backseat, as if Marty and Randy were holding their breaths. Or waiting to take action if Harry gave a signal.

"I understand," Buddy said, his need for a drink so overwhelming that his hands trembled and he dropped them out of sight of the streetlight.

Harry smiled, turned away, and grabbed the steering

wheel, his foot depressing the accelerator. The tires prayed gravel behind them. More silence from the back-seat. After a while, Harry looked over at Buddy. And smiled. A forgiving smile. He hit Buddy playfully on the shoulder.

"You did good tonight, blood," he said. Black again.

Christ, Buddy thought, how did I get mixed up in all this?

Although, he knew, of course, the answer to that question.

The problem with being an eleven-year-old Avenger was just that: being eleven years old and an Avenger. It would have been easier if he were older, like fifteen or sixteen, or old enough to have a driver's license so that he could zoom around easier. He had to depend on his bike, a rickety three-speeder his mother bought him secondhand. He also had to depend on his ingenuity and, of course, his patience. Patience was the watchword, his mother always said, and she should know, she was the most patient person in the world. Washing, scrubbing, dusting. She kept missing her favorite TV shows because there was always something else for her to do around the house. Sewing, cooking, ironing, scrubbing, dusting.

The Avenger had other problems. His shyness, for instance. He was not shy when he was The Avenger, carrying out his acts of revenge. But in the classroom or in the schoolyard, he found it difficult to make friends, to be at ease with the other students. When called upon to recite in class, he blushed furiously, his throat tightening and his voice emerging in a ridiculous squeak. Which made Vaughn Masterson snicker. Vaughn Masterson spent the day snickering. When kids answered questions or went to the blackboard, or received good marks in a test. The

Avenger realized finally that Vaughn snickered because he was jealous. And dumb. D-U-M-B. In capital letters. Cheated when he could. Tried to sneak glances at The Avenger's test papers because The Avenger always received good marks, A's most of the time. Vaughn Masterson sat behind him and poked him in the back. That was mild compared to what he did to the other kids. Took their lunch bags and squished the sandwiches in his hands and threw them to the ground. He would have had some respect for Vaughn Masterson if, for instance, he had eaten the stolen lunches instead of destroying them and humiliating the kids he took them from. Like little Danny Davis, whom Vaughn enjoyed tormenting, day after day. Tripping him, pulling his shirt out of his pants, tweaking his cheeks. Especially in front of the girls. Making fun of Danny Davis while everybody giggled and those who didn't giggle turned away in embarrassment, feeling guilty because they didn't stand up to him. Why didn't they stand up to him? Vaughn wasn't *that* much bigger than anyone else in the fifth grade. But he carried a powerful air with him as he strutted through the schoolyard, a faint smile on his face as if he found the world an amusing place to be.

After observing Vaughn Masterson doing his dirty work for several weeks, The Avenger knew that *something* had to be done. He planned his course of action. He was good at planning. His mother called it daydreaming— you'll dream your life away, she'd say. In those daydreams, he was brave and daring, reckless and adventurous. He dreamed about what he would do to Vaughn Masterson. And how he would do it. He had to be patient, of course, had to wait for the proper conditions, one of the conditions being that it was necessary to obtain the means. And, after obtaining the means, would have to wait awhile—patience again—to let things cool down.

Finally, all the conditions were right and he carried out his scheme. On that particular day, he followed Vaughn home from school. Did not ride his bike, but walked. Did not really walk but scampered behind Vaughn, hiding behind bushes and trees, thrilling, like the movies. When Vaughn arrived home, The Avenger waited across the street, concealing himself in a gazebo on the front lawn. He had noticed the gazebo on an earlier expedition to Vaughn's street. He had observed several other things. That Vaughn Masterson was alone in the afternoon, his parents off working somewhere. The house with the gazebo also was unoccupied in the afternoon. Vaughn would stay in his house for a half hour or so, changing his clothes, having a bite to eat in the kitchen. The Avenger had employed his skills at spying to learn Vaughn's routine.

Finally, Vaughn came out of the house, chewing the last remnants of his peanut butter and jelly sandwich. He had changed into jeans and a faded yellow shirt, his stomach bulging slightly at his belt. Made his way lazily down the steps to the back of the house where, if he followed his usual routine, he would open the garage door and fool around inside for a while. That's exactly what he did now.

The Avenger crossed the street, looking this way and that, to see if anyone was watching. Except for a stray dog sniffing at a car down at the corner, the street was deserted.

Standing a few feet in front of the garage, The Avenger called out: "Hey, Vaughn, how're you doing?"

Vaughn emerged from the garage, squinting into the sun, looking annoyed.

"What do *you* want?" he said, sneering, that *you* snapping with contempt.

"This," The Avenger said, smiling.

From his book bag he removed the revolver he had

stolen from his grandfather. Kneeling, he held the revolver with both hands and pressed the trigger. The lower half of Vaughn's face exploded in bone and blood as the bullet struck. The noise of the shot was deafening and the recoil of the gun sent The Avenger sprawling backward. He fell on his behind, on the hard pavement, pain shooting along his spinal column.

As the echo of the shot faded in the afternoon, The Avenger scrambled to his feet. The smell of sulfur filled the air. His breath came in short gasps as he looked around, listening for neighborhood sounds. All was quiet. Nobody in sight. The dog down the street was gone.

Ignoring the blood and the shattered face, and the pain in his spine, The Avenger went about his business as planned, heart hammering dangerously in his chest. He wiped the handle of the revolver with a piece of Kleenex. The hardest part was placing the revolver in Vaughn's left hand—The Avenger had noticed in school that he was left-handed—and curling Vaughn's index finger around the trigger. He then let the revolver fall out of Vaughn's hand and clatter to the pavement. Just as he had seen it done on television.

Squinting, he looked down at the bloody fallen figure. Vaughn Masterson lay there in a ghastly kind of stillness. A thing, suddenly. He would not bully anyone again, and the kids in the fifth grade of Lucy Peary Elementary School could now go about their business in peace.

The Avenger smiled his smile of vengeance as he picked up his book bag, slung it over his shoulder, and went home. He arrived in time to share with his mother their usual afternoon snack of ice-cold milk and molasses cookies.

* * *

Pink. Bright, cool like a Popsicle. That was the color his year. The color she and Patti and Leslie had chosen as heir motif. They had also decided to be subtle about it, not going wild but using pink in their accessories, alternating between necklaces, bracelets, and earrings. Pink tank tops, a touch of pink in their attire. Also pink thoughts. Which meant not hot. To play it cool with guys. They also used *pink* as a code word. But the word changed to suit the situation. Like with Johnny Taylor. Leslie was *pink* about him. And Patti would giggle, she was a giggler, giggles like bubbles gurgling out of her at the least provocation, which drove some people crazy but not Jane and not Leslie. Best friends put up with such things.

Pink united them in a secret alliance, their use of the word puzzling to others but drawing them together. Leslie, for instance, was the lady of Burnside High, always dressed up like Sunday, fussy with her hair and makeup. Yet, she had this crazy side to her that only Patti and Jane knew about. "Pink him," Leslie would cry out when angry momentarily with some guy. And they all laughed and giggled, knowing the word that Leslie had used *pink* for as a substitute.

Although blue was Jane's favorite color, she went along with the pink delirium, glad to do so because she loved Patti and Leslie, would do anything for them, anything at all, and they felt the same about her.

Until the trashing.

She thought of it as "the trashing" but it was more than that, of course. It was also what happened to Karen and the coma that held her in a strange kind of sleep in ICU at the hospital. Jane tried not to think about that. In her mind she placed it all within the context of one word: *trashing.* Which included her house and her home and everything in it. Karen had been trashed, ruined. Tossed aside, down the cellar stairs, like a rag doll when someone was through playing with it.

The effects of the trashing had spread beyond the house, however, and the ICU. Had changed things. Had changed Arbor Lane and also Patti and Leslie. Oh, they were sympathetic, of course. Stunned at what had happened. They visited the house the day after the trashing, and Jane had led them reluctantly through the rooms, sorry she had invited them to view the damage. Had not actually invited them but had responded to their curiosity as they sat on the back porch. "Is it really as bad as everybody says?" Patti had asked. Who is everybody? Jane wondered. Then, wanting to see the damage through their eyes, Jane ushered them through the house, growing uncomfortable at the sight of the damage and disarray. More than that. *Ashamed* suddenly, wanting to hide somewhere, as if *she* had done something wrong, not the culprits, not the invaders.

Leslie, always the lady, picked her way through the house, nose wrinkled a bit, her arms at awkward angles. What angles? Jane realized that Leslie was trying to avoid touching anything, as if she might somehow become contaminated. Patti, the giggler, did not giggle for once. Which was worse than if she had giggled. Instead, she kept saying: "Wow." Murmuring *wow* again and again, in a breathless whisper until Jane wanted to scream: Pink you!

Later, they sat on the back porch banister, balancing themselves delicately, legs swinging back and forth.

"Who would want to do such a thing?" Leslie said. "I mean, why pick on your house? Why pick on Karen?"

The choice of words offended Jane. *Pick on.*

"The police said Karen was unlucky enough to come home at the wrong moment," Jane said, her voice flat and risp. "It could have been anybody." She felt as though Karen had been criticized.

"Picking your house was certainly bad luck, all right," Patti said.

Picking.

"What about the police?" Patti asked. "What do they think?"

"The police don't know what to think," Jane said, banging her heels against the banister posts. "No clues." *Clues,* a movie word. "No witnesses." Another movie word. Which made it all seem unreal. "That other stuff, the phone calls, the dead squirrel. The police don't think they're connected. They think the trashing was done by someone else, more than one person. Four or five."

"You mean, Karen and four or five guys . . ." Leslie began, horror growing in her eyes, her voice dying away in that horror.

"They're not sure about that," Jane said, avoiding the word that Leslie avoided and then going ahead with it. "Look, she was not raped. She was . . . assaulted, attacked. But even that much is hard to tell. She fell down the stairs. Or was pushed down the stairs. But definitely not raped." That hateful terrible word again.

No one spoke for a while. A stillness pervaded the neighborhood except for the distant purring of a lawn mower. Jane wanted to change the subject but also needed to break the silence in which that terrible word seemed to echo.

"The police are puzzled about how they entered the house," Jane said. "There was what they called 'no signs of forced entry.' " Seeing their puzzled expressions, she said: "Which means, they didn't break down the doors to get in. Or didn't pry them open." Then, almost to herself, because it was so puzzling: "Another thing, they didn't break any windows. Broke like a thousand glasses and all the mirror in the house but no windows. . . ."

"What does that mean?" Patti asked, perplexed.

"I don't know," Jane said, her voice sounding distan and meek.

Their shoes drummed against the banister. "I used to love it here," Jane said. "Arbor Lane." Her voice wistful a she whispered the name of the street. After the initial re sentment over her father's transfer to Burnside had sub sided, she had been fascinated by Arbor Lane and her nev neighborhood, realizing that it was a dream street, lik something out of *Leave It to Beaver* in the old televisio reruns. Neat houses, with shutters and rose arbors, bird baths on front lawns, and the lawns carefully manicure People waving hello to each other, evening barbecues i backyards and the aroma of burning charcoal or woo smoke from chimneys. A neighborhood of station wagon and vans, family cars. Kids of all ages and sizes. Typica kids, some regular, some nerds. But then all kids just be fore reaching puberty seemed to have undergone som kind of brat injection. Like her brother, Artie, and his ad diction to video games, barricading himself in his roon while he zipped and zapped at the television set, causin his father to issue ultimatums and limits on playing th games. Mikey Bryan from two houses down who special ized in riding his bike helter-skelter on the sidewalk, run ning people down unless they leaped out of the way. Littl Kenny Crane whom everyone picked on. Every neighbor hood had a kid like that and Kenny Crane with his bab face and sissy walk filled the role on Arbor Lane. She onc saw Artie, who wasn't exactly her idea of a hero, defen Kenny, telling the other kids to leave him alone, placing hi arm around Kenny Crane's frail shoulders. Maybe ther was hope for Artie, after all.

"Hi, Jane."

She looked up to see Amos Dalton trudging by, taking a shortcut through the backyard. Amos: an old man's name and the boy himself like a premature middle-aged man. Always a worried look on his face, always carrying one or two library books. Always sly glances at Jane's boobs. She was self-conscious about her breasts these days and boys staring at them all the time. She was both proud of them—they seemed to have appeared practically overnight—and embarrassed about them. Wanted them and didn't want them. Wished she could flaunt them the way Karen flaunted hers.

She crossed her arms in front of her chest now as Amos stopped below.

"Sorry about your house," he said in a croaking voice. "And your sister."

She nodded, hoping he'd just go away.

"If there's anything I can do, just let me know," he said, scuffing the grass with his foot. He didn't wear sneakers like other kids but laced shoes, middle-aged shoes.

"Who was *that*?" Leslie asked, face wrinkled in disgust as Amos trudged away.

"A kid from the neighborhood," Jane replied. "He's kind of weird but nice." Trying to hide her irritation, wanting to defend Amos, the neighborhood, herself.

"Oh, oh," Patti said. "Speaking of weird . . ."

They looked up to see Mickey Looney getting out of his old beat-up truck. Mickey was the neighborhood handyman, performing odd jobs, mowing lawns, shoveling snow, raking leaves, all in season. His old truck wheezed and rattled as it gasped its way through the streets. Short and plump, ageless, he could have been thirty years old or fifty.

"Who is he?" Leslie asked, as if she were at a zoo inquiring about some strange species.

"His name is Mickey Stallings but everybody calls him Mickey Looney," she said. "Behind his back of course." Needing to explain: "Because he looks like that old movie star, Mickey Rooney? But, Looney because he is sort of odd."

She was sorry she had told them about Mickey's nickname as soon as the words were out of her mouth. In the neighborhood, the nickname Mickey Looney was used affectionately for this gentle man who patted dogs, tousled the hair of small kids, nodded respectfully to the men and tipped his faded baseball cap to the ladies.

"He gives me the creeps," Leslie said.

"Me too," Patti agreed.

"He's very nice," Jane said, anger stirring inside her. Anger at Patti and Leslie and also at herself. "He's smart, too. Knows how to fix things, knows all about plants and stuff. My father says he could have been an engineer if he'd gone to college. But he likes fixing things, working for himself. . ."

Patti rolled her eyes. Jane knew that look. It meant: Are you kidding?

"I still think he's weird," Patti said.

Jane felt like a traitor. To her house, which she had exposed to Patti and Leslie. To Mickey Looney, who was not really loony at all. She had betrayed Mickey, her house, the entire neighborhood.

Now the silence again as they watched Mickey unloading his garden equipment, silence thick and heavy like an invisible fog enveloping them all. Jane sighed, softly but tremulously, hoping that Leslie and Patti did not notice. Loneliness invaded her. Here she was, sitting on the porch banister of her house with her two best friends in the whole wide world, and she had never felt so alone, so forlorn, in all her life.

Buddy placed the pint bottle on the top of his father's workbench in the garage and carefully studied the label, *Seagram's Gin, 80 Proof,* then took the bottle in his hands and caressed it tenderly, as if it contained something precious. Which it did, of course. Actually, he hated the taste of the stuff. Despite its perfumey taste, it burned his throat and spread sourness in his stomach. He much preferred Coke, Classic. But Classic Coke did not do to him what gin did. Even when he mixed the gin with the Coke it did not take away the harsh edges of things, did not blur, did not bring the haziness, did not soothe him with soft strokings, letting him float pleasantly away while just sitting there. Two or three gulps and he would give himself up to sweet lassitude, and the hate and the ache folded their tents like the Arabs and silently stole away.

That's what was happening now, all the rotten things stealing away—this terrible house that was his home and that other house where the girl had bounced sickeningly down the stairs—replaced by a glow spreading through his limbs, as if his body were a light bulb on low intensity.

He glanced around the garage which his father never used for cars but for storing the paraphernalia of house maintenance—lawn mower, wheelbarrow, shovels and rakes, all kinds of tools spread haphazardly here and there, which made it easy to hide the bottles of booze Buddy sneaked into the place. Neatness was not one of his father's strong points. He always left a trail of disarray and debris behind him. Kept losing things. Didn't hang up his clothes. Ironic: in this house, the son was neater than the father. The mother would nag his father to put things away, holding the son up as a model.

Notice the formality here: calling them Mother and Father, not Mom and Dad. No more Hi Mom, Hi Dad, how did things go today? What's on for dinner? Pork chops? Swell. We all love pork chops. And then telling jokes at the dinner table, like we always do. Dad's atrocious talking-animal jokes which were funny without being funny. Like the kangaroo who orders Scotch on the rocks at the bar and . . .

Christ.

Not only didn't call them Mom or Dad anymore. Did not call them anything at all. Not even *hey.* Amend that. Called his mother *Mom* sometimes because it slipped out from habit. She still lived here at least. He had a soft spot for her but was angry with her, too. But it wasn't her fault at all, Addy said. But what did Addy know? Addy Walker, fifteen years old. Little sister but not so little, slightly overweight. Not particularly likable, either. Pain in the ass, in fact. Little Miss Know-It-All. Sometimes he almost hated her, her smarty-pants attitude, high honor roll, smirking as they compared report cards, Buddy barely managing to keep a B average, always in danger of flunking at least one subject, never acing anything. Addy was starring in the sophomore play, a play she had written with her English teacher, for crissakes. While he had even flunked basketball, hairline fracture of his knee ending potential stardom. Stardom? Hell, he had been lucky they let him sit on the bench: too short at five nine in a game that called for giants, too uncoordinated, with a knee that gave way on occasion, sending him unceremoniously to the floor.

Have another drink, Buddy.

He lifted the bottle to his lips, then hesitated. The moment always came when one more swallow was too much, made him cross the border between being pleasantly high and deathly sick and he never knew when that moment would come, which swallow would change things

around. Like at that girl's house the other night. One minute, beautiful. Next minute, sick on the floor. Vomiting on
the rug of a perfect stranger.

He drank anyway but a small, tentative swallow. Testing, testing. Testing the state of his stomach, the state of his
life. As he swallowed he heard the back door open and
then slam shut. Glancing hazily at his watch, he saw that it
was two thirty-three. Addy home from school. Unexpected:
she usually stayed late, involved in all kinds of extracurric-
ular stuff. His mother worked at the office till five, never
got home till almost six.

Buddy sat still. Gathered himself. Blinked, relaxed.
Slipped the bottle of booze under the pile of stuff on the
workbench. He rose slowly to his feet, pleased to see that
he was only a bit dizzy. He had found out since he had
started to drink that he was a superb actor, that he could
have stolen the show even in Addy's stupid play. He was
often a bit high, a bit drunk, but nobody noticed. Maybe
Addy did. She often regarded him curiously, scrutinizing
him as if he were a puzzle she could not solve.

"How much do you drink?" she had asked one night,
meeting him in the hallway upstairs.

Her question stunned him for a moment, almost made
him lose his cool. Not *do you drink*? But *how much do you
drink*?

"Not much," he managed to mutter as he brushed by
her.

So, he was always extra careful in her presence, tried
to avoid her most of the time, which was hard sometimes
because she seemed to be trying to track him down.

It was different with other people, especially teachers.
He found that if you were polite, didn't say very much,
chewed peppermints or Life Savers or gum—all of which
he actually hated—you could fake your way through any

number of situations. The trick, too, was knowing when not to take that extra swallow: like now. He had stopped at the right moment, Addy arriving home unexpectedly.

The door between the garage and the back hall opened. Addy stuck her head in. Clown face, round, sprinkled with freckles. She would never win a beauty contest.

"What are you doing?" she inquired suspiciously, looking around the garage. "God, you're acting spooky lately."

"All of us are," he replied. The secret: short sentences.

"You're weirdest of all," she said. Frowning, she said: "Have you been drinking?" Sniffing the air.

He had failed to pop anything in his mouth, had not anticipated Addy searching him out in the garage. Now, he pressed his lips together, tried to breathe through his nostrils. Made himself busy at the bench, as if he was looking for something.

"Mind your own business," he said, enunciating each word separately to let her know he really meant for her to mind her own business.

Funny thing: most of the time, they each minded their own business. Days passed when they hardly communicated. The good old days, that is. Not lately, not in these bad new days. These days, Addy tracked him down, popped in the house early from school. Like today, this afternoon.

"I hope you're not drinking *and* driving," Addy said. "That would be the most stupid thing in the world."

"I don't drink and drive," Buddy said. Which was true. His license had been issued only seven weeks ago and Buddy had vowed never to drive while liquor flowed through his veins. This took an effort of will because his mother kept offering him the use of the car. Guilt, on her part, probably, trying to compensate for the dismal thing their lives had become. Buddy was not very proud of himself these days but he was proud about keeping his vow even though the car, sitting day after day in the driveway, was a constant temptation.

Addy studied him closely now, eyes narrowed in appraisal. "I have a feeling you're drunk right this minute," she said.

"I'm not drunk," he declared, bringing himself to his full height, which wasn't much, really.

She looked at him for a terrible moment, her dark eyes flashing darker than ever, and then turned away, slamming the door behind her as she dashed out of the place.

Buddy grimaced, realized he'd been holding his breath. He let the breath out. That terrible look in her eyes. They had always shot dynamite glances at each other when they weren't being completely indifferent, Addy dismayed at his lackadaisical ways, his lack of ambition, the way he bumped into things. He could not abide her schedules, her snap-crackle-and-pop way of doing things, always on time, on the ball. He was far from stupid but Addy made him look stupid, feel stupid.

Leaning against the workbench, resisting another swallow of gin, he tried to bring back her expression, the way she had looked at him a moment before abandoning the garage. That look. Not only disgust at his drinking but something else.

In the downstairs bathroom, he brushed his teeth with Crest, gulped Scope, gargled, hoping that the smell of gin had been obliterated. He went upstairs, listened at the landing, heard nothing. In the second-floor hallway, he saw that her bedroom door was closed. Not unusual. Neither was the absence of sound. Addy hated the radio, couldn't stand rock music or anything resembling contemporary stuff while studying. Buddy could not face homework or a theme paper without Bruce Springsteen or somebody to help him along.

He knocked at her door, softly. *What am I doing?* Knocked again. *I should be glad she's in there and I'm out here.*

"What do you want?" she asked, voice muffled.

"I don't know," he said. Which was exactly right.

"Stupid," she called out. Her voice sounded funny. Not funny, but broken.

He stood there. Waited. What was he waiting for?

She opened the door, slowly, letting it swing wide open before appearing. Her face, when he finally saw it, was red and shining. Eyes wet. She sniffed, blew her nose with a Kleenex.

She'd been crying, for crissakes.

"You've been crying?" he said.

"You're so observant," she replied. Sarcastically, of course.

And suddenly he, too, felt like crying.

Because he saw himself and Addy for what they were: two kids whose parents were divorcing, living in a house where nobody loved anybody else anymore.

While a bruised and battered girl lay in a hospital somewhere.

"Come in," she said.

But he could not go in. He stared at her for a long moment and then turned away, dashed down the stairs, through the front hallway and out of the house, not realizing he was running until he found himself a block away on Oak Avenue heading nowhere.

While Karen slept.

Deep in her dreams—or did she dream? Or even sleep?

Jane wondered about the strange place Karen now occupied, between life and death: alive but not alive, sleeping but not sleeping.

Karen was seldom alone in that hospital room. Someone in the family remained with her almost all the time, except the late nighttime hours. Jane's mother kept vigil in the morning and Jane often joined her in the afternoon after school. Her father and mother sat beside Karen's bed in the evenings, sometimes together, sometimes alternating with each other. Jane dropped in at the hospital at odd hours, not only after school but on her way home from the Mall or from a movie and sometimes found her father, sometimes Artie, there. The family had no formal visiting plan. The ceaseless routine of visiting had developed naturally, became a habit around which the rest of their lives centered.

One day, Jane found herself alone in the hospital room and it seemed to her that Karen was sinking, deeper and deeper into that strange terrible sleep, her body slight and slender under the sheet. Occasionally, she moved, twitched, sudden involuntary movements that, for one split second, brought a flash of hope. Then, nothing, the stillness again.

The doctor had encouraged the family to talk to Karen but Jane found it hard to do that. Just as she had found it hard to communicate with Karen at home. Although Karen was two years younger, Jane did not feel like her older sister. Karen glided easily through life, popular at school, adjusting quickly to Burnside, the telephone ringing constantly for her only a few days after the family had moved from Monument. Secretly, Jane regarded Karen as a snob, immersed in her social life at school, ignoring her parents as well as Artie and Jane herself, acknowledging Jane's existence only when she invaded her room to borrow, without asking, her clothes, her cologne, her jewelry. Which provided arguments and accusations.

"Why does she act like I don't even exist and then borrows my things?" Jane had asked her mother.

"Maybe she envies you."

"Me? She's the one with a million friends, has such a flair for style . . ."

"Yes, but you have taste, Jane," her mother said. "Remember, she's younger, she looks up to you. That's why she borrows your things. . . ."

"Then why doesn't she just ask me? Instead of going behind my back . . ."

"She's shy . . ."

Karen shy?

"People are not always what they seem to be," her mother said, using one of those mysterious sayings parents rely on to end conversations at a convenient moment.

Regarding Karen in the bed, looking vulnerable and, yes, shy and unguarded, Jane said, "I'm sorry," her voice too loud in the quiet room where the small *beep* of the monitor was the only other sound.

"If you envied me, maybe I was jealous of you," Jane admitted, hoping that Karen *could* hear her words. "Please come out of this, Karen, so we can talk about it, do something about it . . ."

The echo of her voice died out, along with the odd but somehow comforting words she had spoken to her silent sister.

While Karen slept in that high hospital bed, the house underwent repairs. A sophisticated alarm system, connected with police headquarters, was installed. New furniture was purchased plus three television sets, a CD set, and two VCRs. Her mother also bought new bedding—sheets and blankets to replace those that had been torn to shreds by the invaders. Her mother, in fact, went on a sad kind of shopping spree, replacing things that she thought the trashers had even *touched*. Particularly clothes. She and Jane went to the Mall and bought tops and skirts—and she brought home new shirts and underwear for Jane's father. Meanwhile, the repairs were completed in record time as the workmen performed with urgency, working overtime willingly, as if they knew it was important to obliterate all evidence of mischief as soon as possible. *Mischief.* That was the word used by a man named Stoddard, a friend of Jane's father who was boss of the work crew. He kept muttering the word under his breath as he directed the repairs and performed along with the crew as they scrubbed and painted and replaced.

Within a week, the house was restored to what passed for normal. Everything bright and new. The old wallpaper had been removed from Jane's room and she decided to have the walls painted, choosing white instead of her favorite blue. Blue was spoiled for her forever and so, in a way, was pink. She did not replace her posters but allowed the walls to remain uncluttered, untouched, pure. She wasn't quite sure that *pure* was the right word but it suited the room somehow.

The smell of paint lingered in the air after the workmen's departure, along with other smells Jane could not identify, probably turpentine or the liquid wax on the floors. But something else, too.

"The smell of newness," her mother said, sniffing the air, making her voice light and bright.

"That's right," Jane said, forcing brightness into her own voice, wondering if her mother also was playacting, whether her mother could detect that other smell, the smell that persisted, rising to her nostrils on occasion, lurking under all the new smells. She was aware of the smell when she entered her bedroom, a soiled scent just barely there, making her pause and sniff tentatively, wrinkling her nose. The smell of something spoiled and decayed, an under-the-surface odor, hinting of vomit and things gone bad. Faint, yes, but unmistakable, not always there but coming and going, elusive sometimes, but other times strong, overpowering. She avoided looking at the spot near the door where she had encountered that puddle of vomit. To her surprise—and horror—she began to detect that elusive smell elsewhere, catching a drifting whiff when she was on the bus going to school, on the sidewalk in front of the Mall, in the classroom once, the smell suddenly stronger than schoolroom chalk. She would sniff cautiously and sometimes the smell evaporated, disappeared at once or lingered for a while, tantalizing in a horrible way. She wondered, a bit panicky, if the odor came from herself, if somehow it was being manufactured by her body, created out of her own horror at what had happened. She began to douse herself with cologne, applied creams and salves, sought out the strongest deodorants to rub into her armpits. She began to hold herself aloof from people, not letting anyone come too close, leaning over awkwardly when she kissed her mother and father good night. Sometimes, she caught her mother looking at her peculiarly and quickly turned away or left the room or began to jabber like a madwoman. And sometimes she caught her mother's own face lost in deep thought or sadness and wanted to reach out to her, cry out, touch her or fling herself in her arms. But could not, could not, always holding back.

And all the while Karen slept.

It wasn't only that foul odor, that terrible smell, but the house itself that began to bother Jane. She started fleeing the place, finding excuses not to be there. After visiting the hospital, she sometimes took the bus to downtown

Wickburg and wandered the Mall, killing time, going in and out of the stores, trying on jackets and skirts, drinking a 7-Up. She did not stay too long in the stores or linger on the plastic benches near the fountain, did not want to give the appearance of being a stray, homeless. At home, she quickly changed and roamed the neighborhood or simply hung out in the backyard. She didn't seek out the company of the other girls on the street because she wasn't in a mood for polite conversation or talk about clothes or makeup or movies and television. She wished she were a writer or a painter or a musician so that she could lose herself in some form of creativity, express the emotions that stirred inside her. What emotions? She felt as though she were fooling herself because she felt no emotions, really. Felt dead inside. Empty. Like a vessel waiting to be filled. Filled with what? She didn't know.

Her father called a family meeting one night. He did not issue special invitations but somehow let them all know that they should gather in the living room after supper. He faced them, standing self-consciously at the fireplace, frowning. Jane wondered whether he had a headache because he kept rubbing his forehead.

"I'm going to make a speech," he said. "A short one. But your mother and I feel that certain things should be said."

If her mother was in on the plan, then that meant the speech was really being made to an audience of two, her and her brother, Artie.

"We can't pretend that the vandalism didn't take place," he said, voice strained as if he had been shouting against the wind all day. "But we have to go on living. Living here, in this house. We have to put it all behind us. Not as if it didn't happen but looking ahead instead of behind us. We also can't pretend that Karen isn't in the hospital. In a . . ." His voice faltered and he skipped the word *coma,* after pausing for a minute. "So we have to be concerned about her, think about her, pray for her, and visit her. Which we've all been doing and which we must and will continue to do. But we also have to get on with our own lives. We can't afford to be bitter, to let what happened spoil our lives."

He took a deep breath and paused. "Now let me talk about something we've all avoided talking about. The trashers themselves.

"We don't know why they did what they did. Why they chose our house. Everybody, and that includes the police, thinks it was a random thing, that we shouldn't feel as though we were special targets, that it was a personal attack on us as a family. The world is filled with weird people and some of those weird people came upon our house and did terrible things. We can't deny that it happened but we have to get over it. The trashers would be the big winners if we let what they did change us, spoil our lives. Yes, Karen is in the hospital. But she's alive and the doctors are optimistic about her chances of recovery. The police are convinced that she was what they call an unintended victim. That the trashers were attacking the house, not her, not us. We have to believe that and get on with our lives."

Such a brave speech, delivered with such determination and resolution that Jane wanted to rush to him and embrace him.

After that, she and her family settled into a kind of a routine, caught up in busy days and evenings. Her father left for work every day as usual, spent long hours at the office and the rest of the time at the hospital. He did not play golf anymore on weekends. Her mother acted as if someone had cranked her up in the morning and dispatched her on her daily rounds. She was a whirlwind of bustling activity, dashing between home and the hospital meanwhile doing the housework, cleaning, dusting, knitting, seldom pausing to catch her breath. All of which made Jane wonder: Was all of this normal? What was normal, anyway?

She developed her own routine in the neighborhood. Sometimes, she did not feel like taking the bus trip to Wickburg, and found the house lonely and forlorn. She'd put on her Nikes and shorts and jog the streets, dodging the bike brigade and the brats, ignoring them when they whistled and yelled or tried to sideswipe her. The kids were pests but she preferred them to that silent empty house.

"Hello, Jane."

She paused in her jogging as Mickey Looney tipped his baseball hat.

Jane drew up, breathing heavily, glad for the respite. She was not the most athletic of persons, probably the least.

"Hi, Mickey," she said. He blushed when anyone looked directly at him, deep crimson sweeping his face.

"Almost time to plant tomatoes?" she asked.

"Thirtieth of May," Mickey said, seriously, suddenly, the professional planter. "Anytime before then is too early, New England being what it is."

He seemed to hesitate, then kicked at something invisible on the ground. "How's Karen?" he asked. "I've been meaning to inquire but don't like to intrude."

"She's still in the coma," Jane said. Observing how stricken he looked, she reassured him: "She's not suffering, Mickey, and she's not any worse."

"I hope she'll come out of it," he said, still kicking at nothing.

Weird Amos Dalton came along, his arms loaded with books as usual. He did not look up as he trudged by.

"Hey, Amos," Jane called on an impulse. "What're you reading?"

Amos looked up with a pained expression as if it hurt him to encounter someone face-to-face. "What do you want to know for?" he asked.

"Just curious."

Mickey said: "I don't read so much since we got television."

Weird, Jane thought. Television began thirty, forty years ago.

"Television is for morons," Amos said, a middle-aged scowl on his face.

Mickey recoiled, stepping backward. "*Jeopardy!*'s my favorite program," he said, not looking at Jane. Or Amos.

"Hey, Amos," Jane said, "I watch television. Millions of people watch it. We're not all morons. I like *Jeopardy!* too."

Amos hugged his books closer to his chest. Turned away, then turned back, grimacing. "I hope your sister's getting better," he said, his voice rusty, as if it hurt him to speak.

Still clutching his books, Amos marched away, a lonesome parade of one, while Mickey began to fuss with his tools at the back of the truck.

"Time to go to work," he said, tugging at his baseball cap.

Jane resumed jogging, not really jogging but a quick-step kind of walking. Going down the street and turning the corner, she felt somehow cheered up by the meeting with these odd people. Maybe because the man and the boy, both so very different, had mentioned Karen. Everyone else avoided speaking about her, as if she had ceased to exist, had passed out of people's lives.

She herself had passed out of people's lives. She seldom saw Patti or Leslie anymore. They nodded when they met in the corridors at school and sometimes endured awkward lunch hours at the same table, the conversation stilted and superficial, broken by prolonged silences. Jane did not blame them for not continuing the friendship they had enjoyed, if indeed it had been friendship. She was the one who had first withdrawn, avoiding them, sensing that she had become an embarrassment, a feeling that began that morning on the porch. Her separation from Patti and Leslie meant that she did not have to playact anymore, did not have to pretend that everything was fine, did not have to be on the defensive about her house and family and Karen. Yet, sometimes, when she saw the two girls walking down the corridor, easy with each other, laughing, casual, she was filled with a longing, a yearning for—she was not sure what—perhaps simply a friend to talk to.

But all of this was minor, of course, compared with what had happened to Karen, although sometimes she almost envied Karen as she slept on that high hospital bed.

The death of Vaughn Masterson was reported as an accident in the newspaper. The story noted that the weapon had been stolen from the apartment of retired police sergeant Louis Kendrick a month earlier. Allowing the victim the benefit of the doubt, police deduced that the boy probably found the weapon after it had been either lost or discarded by the thief. Vaughn Masterson evidently took the weapon home, hid it away somewhere in his house or in his father's garage, and had taken it out to play with on that fatal day, not realizing it was loaded. The boy died instantly when the weapon was discharged. The newspaper did not sensationalize the story, ran the boy's picture—one taken by a school photographer the year before—but did not go into great detail about the fatal shooting.

The Avenger read the story avidly, his heart pumping joyously, his eyes bright and his head warm as if he had a fever. But a nice fever. He studied Vaughn's face in the picture, his neatly combed hair, the big smile that revealed small sharp teeth.

Although he felt an immense satisfaction as he read the story, he did not make the mistake of cutting it out of the newspaper, to save as a souvenir. He had seen a movie in which the killer was apprehended when a yellowed newspaper clipping about the murder was found years later in his attic.

The entire fifth grade attended the funeral at the First Congregational church. The Avenger was amazed at the hypocrisy of his classmates, especially the girls who cried and sniffled and blew their noses. Even the guys—and Danny Davis in particular—looked sad. The Avenger arranged his face in what he considered a mournful expression. Although he hated doing this, he knew that he could not afford to stand out in the crowd, could not draw attention to himself.

Vaughn's parents walked down the aisle a moment before the coffin was wheeled in. The Avenger felt a tug of sympathy, picturing his own mother in church if he should die. In a way, The Avenger felt sorry for Vaughn's parents as they sat down in the pew. Mr. Masterson's hand trembled as he placed his arm around Mrs. Masterson's shoulder. Chances were they did not know what a terrible person their son had been. No wonder they were sad. The Avenger realized he had done them a favor by killing him before he grew up to disgrace them. The Avenger was convinced that Vaughn Masterson would have grown up to be a terrible person.

The minister began to speak. Like a teacher in school, speaking softly and slowly as if he was going to pass out a test at the end of the sermon. He spoke about eternity and goodness and living one's life in the glow of the Lord. He spoke of the tragedy of an early death but the glory of going to the Lord without a tarnished soul.

The Avenger barely listened as he kept his eye on the gleaming wood of Vaughn's coffin. The minister said we should be thankful for Vaughn's time with us on earth. The Avenger was also thankful for Vaughn Masterson. He had shown The Avenger how easy it was to get rid of someone who did not deserve to live. Easier than on television, where the murderers always got caught before the final commercial was shown. *Why had it been easy?* The Avenger frowned, seeking an answer as the minister droned on. Why hadn't the police caught him? Two policemen had visited the school and talked to everyone. Asking questions. Had Vaughn been acting strange recently? Had anyone seen him with the gun?

When his turn came, The Avenger had looked them straight in the eye and lied. No, he had not seen Vaughn Masterson after school on the day he died. He learned that it was easy to lie, easier than reciting lessons in class. In movies and TV, the guilty party always looked guilty, sweating, not looking anyone in the eye. But The Avenger answered their questions in his best helpful voice, like when he asked his mother if she wanted him to run an errand even when he did not feel like running an errand.

As he yawned with boredom, trying to tune out the minister, The Avenger made a startling discovery. The discovery came when the minister said: "No one knows why Vaughn had to die that afternoon." The words banged around in The Avenger's head. *No one knows why. Why.* In other words, neither the police nor anyone else knew the reason for the killing, the motive. He seized on that word *motive.* He had heard that word a million times in movies and television—*once we know the motive, we will find the killer*—but never realized its deep meaning until this moment. The motive is what links the killer with the victim. The motive is the arrow that points toward the killer. If the motive can't be found, then the killer can't be found. Simple. Terrific. That's why they couldn't connect anyone with Vaughn Masterson's murder and why they did not even know that it *was* a murder.

Remember that the next time, he told himself as the minister finally shut up and the organ boomed forth, the pews trembling with the vibrations.

The Avenger found it hard not to smile and had to cover his mouth with his hands as everyone stood up to watch Vaughn Masterson's coffin roll by.

Buddy dreaded dinnertimes. That's because his mother insisted that he and Addy show up at the table at six-fifteen on the dot: "The least we can do is get together once a day."

She was sleek and stylish, every hair in place, slim and elegant. When preparing meals in the kitchen or baking a cake, she never appeared disheveled, never a dab of flour on her face. Even her aprons were stylish, not merely to protect her from spills or splashes. They matched whatever she was wearing.

The dinners were excruciating. The food was not exactly a thing of inspiration either. Because she worked five days a week in downtown Wickburg as an executive secretary, his mother prepared casseroles ahead of time and heated them in the microwave oven. Casseroles or frozen dinners, low-cholesterol, low-calorie meals. She made up for this on weekends when she prepared special dishes following exotic recipes from her collection of cookbooks. She was experimenting with ginger these days. All these crazy dishes, Japanese especially, laced with ginger, which Buddy ate without enthusiasm or dislike, going through the motions like everything else in his life. Addy chewed away listlessly; food was never an exciting thing for her. "I live the life of the spirit," she was fond of saying, although Buddy found about a thousand candy bar wrappers when he went into her room one day looking for a dictionary for his homework.

Food aside, the dinners consisted of chitchat between his mother and Addy, nonstop, as if fines would be handed out if a silence fell. Chatter. About school and work and the weather and traffic conditions, for crissakes. Buddy tuned them out. Which was easy to do when you were in the glow of the gin.

He wondered what would happen if he disturbed the dinnertime routine. Like showing them the story Randy Pierce clipped from the newspaper.

HOUSE VANDALIZED

GIRL, 14, INJURED

See what your son has been doing, Mom, dear ol' Mom? Keeping busy, but not keeping out of mischief. Randy had made Xerox copies of the news story and spread them around the school, even thumbtacking them up on bulletin boards and on lockers until Harry, his voice withering in its fury, ordered him to take them down. "We don't call attention to ourselves." No more trashing, Buddy had finally said to Harry. Your wish is my command, Harry had replied, bowing low, like an actor on a stage. Harry, the actor, only pretending to give in, as Buddy learned later.

At the dinner table, Buddy was the actor and maybe his mother and Addy were also acting. Pretending that the chair across from their mother was occupied. The empty chair and the lack of plates and utensils. One afternoon,

Buddy looked into the dining room as Addy was setting the table, saw her burst into tears and realized what she had done. Out of an old habit, she had laid out a plate, a knife, fork, and spoon at her father's place. Her face hideous with grief, she swiveled away from him.

"Stop it," Buddy said, voice harsher than he intended. "He isn't worth crying over."

Buddy hated the dining room because it was the place where his father announced that he was moving out of their lives. The announcement, while surprising as well as shocking, made something click inside Buddy and suddenly solved a lot of puzzling things going on in their lives. For weeks, his father had been abstracted, quiet at the table, not participating in the usual dinnertime talk. He was often late for meals, rushing in at the last minute, suddenly talking too loudly, making too many excuses. All of which had been only mildly puzzling to Buddy. Until his father made his big announcement. Apologetic, frowning, clearing his throat, hands moving everywhere, touching his plate, knife, fork, wineglass so that the chardonnay swirled inside and almost overflowed the rim.

"Your mother and I have decided that I should move out of the house for a while," he said in a strangled voice. Which Buddy learned later contained some untruths. First of all, it was his father's own decision: his mother had nothing to do with it. And it wasn't "for a while." He was not planning to come back.

"Are you going to move in with that woman?" Addy asked.

This was the real shock to Buddy, realizing that Addy had known about the woman all along. So shocking that he could not remember later what his father had replied or whether his father, too, had been shocked by Addy's words. Those words later hung in his mind, like washing on a clothesline, whipped by the wind, the words lashing around, echoing: *that woman.* What woman?

"Look, I'm sorry, kids. I didn't want to tell you this way. But there was no good way to tell you." Looking down at his plate, avoiding their eyes. "Yes, there's a woman involved. But I'm not moving in with her. And this is not something I planned. It just happened."

Buddy shot a careful secret glance at his mother. How was she taking this? She was holding herself rigid as if posing for a picture. Her hands folded on the table in front of her, food untouched. Not looking at his father or at Addy or him. Staring off into space, trancelike, as if she were lending her body to the scene but she, herself, her essence, whatever she was, not there at all, absent, gone off somewhere because the words were too terrible to bear.

"Buddy, Addy—I love the two of you," his father continued. "You both know that, I shouldn't have to say it. But I'm saying it anyway. What has happened between your mother and me has nothing to do with you or my love for you."

Later, of course, Addy answered his arguments, refuted them all.

"Did you hear what he said? And how he said it?" Mimicking him: " '*Your mother and I have decided.*' " Snorting: "*He* decided. Mom decided nothing. He wants this woman and he's moved out to be with her, no matter what Mom thinks, no matter what we think." Mimicking him again: " '*What has happened between your mother and me has nothing to do with you.*' " Flinging herself on the bed. "Bullshit. Who does he think it has to do with? Other people? It took the two of them to bring us into the world, didn't it? And now, all of a sudden, what happens to them has nothing to do with *us*? It has everything to do with us.

What happens to them, happens to us. Affects us. Changes our lives."

Buddy was still unprepared, felt stupid, didn't know what to say. "Who's this other woman, Addy?"

"First of all, she's not a woman. She's almost a girl. I mean, Mom is a woman. This . . . this person is maybe in her twenties. I don't know her name." She sat up in the bed, grimacing, face getting red. "Okay, I hate to admit this but I knew about this woman, girl, whatever, because I listened in, eavesdropped on Mom and Dad arguing one night. Felt like a creep standing outside their bedroom, my ear practically glued to the door. Her name is Fay. She's a secretary at his office. Know all those late nights he worked? That's when it started." Again, cruelly mimicking their father, " 'We didn't mean to fall in love.' " Imagine, telling that to Mom. Telling Mom he fell in love with someone else. The bastard . . ." She pulled a blanket around her as if for protection.

Later, his mother knocked at his bedroom door.

"I'm sorry," she said, standing in the doorway, as if unsure of her welcome.

"It's not your fault, Mom," he said, although later he was not thoroughly convinced about whose fault it was.

"I'm also sorry for the way he told you and Addy. That *was* my fault. I wanted to be there when he told you. Wanted to hear him say it. Which was cruel of me, perhaps, but I did it anyway."

Buddy did not know what to say. Wanted to say a lot of things, ask a lot of questions but said nothing. Saw the grief in his mother's face, more than grief, a stunned shocked expression as if she had just heard that the world would end in ten minutes and everybody would perish, all she held dear. Stricken by that look, his mother's shattered eyes, he turned away from her.

"Look, Buddy, I'm not going to make excuses for your father. I don't know what's going to happen. I don't know whether this is temporary or not. Whether he'll get over it. I don't even know if I want him to come back if he *does* get over it. Christ, I don't know anything. . . ."

He had never heard his mother swear before. She was always fastidious, elegant, cool, precise. Or maybe she hadn't sworn. Maybe *Christ* had been the beginning of a prayer.

"He's your father, Buddy. Yours and Addy's. You belong to him as much as you belong to me, as much as either of you can belong to anybody. I want you and Addy to love him. . . ."

But how are we supposed to love him after this? Buddy wondered. Thinking of his father with someone else, another woman, and shutting them out of his life, walking out on them this way, deserting them. And nothing he could do about it.

The next night he met Harry Flowers and his stooges at the Mall.

And got drunk for the first time in his life.

He had made his way to the Mall through a series of bus transfers and hitches. The hitches were time-killers between buses, filling small gaps of space. He arrived downtown at dusk and entered the Mall, where it was never dusk or dawn, afternoon or evening but a world without seasons, without weather.

He sat on a yellow plastic bench, looking at the fountain that did not work anymore but not really seeing it. Not seeing anything. Not wanting to see anything but unable, after a while, to ignore people coming and going, drifting by. Guys and girls holding hands or brushing against each other. Felt sad watching them and did not know why this

sadness should be added to the other sadness that had
brought him to this place.

A couple walked by, holding hands: the girl with long,
flowing blond hair and the guy tall, a basketball type.
Stopped walking and embraced suddenly, as if they were
alone on the planet. Would they someday marry, have kids,
two kids maybe, and then separate and later get divorced?

"Somebody die?"

Buddy heard the words at the same time as he raised
his head and saw Harry Flowers looking down at him. *Is he
talking to me?* Buddy recognized him immediately. Harry
Flowers—one of the popular guys at Wickburg Regional
and also the subject of rumors: drugs, drinking, wild times.

"You *look* like somebody died," Harry said, speaking
unmistakably now to Buddy. "I've been watching you
awhile—you're from school, right?"

Buddy nodded, getting to his feet. Harry Flowers was
about Buddy's height but seemed taller because he stood
almost at attention but at the same time, managed to be
completely at ease. His eyes were the color of khaki,
hooded sometimes but other times, like at this moment,
sympathetic. Buddy had seen him strolling the corridors at
school, always surrounded by his friends, laughing easily,
never hurrying to class like other guys.

"You okay?" Harry asked.

"Nobody died," Buddy answered, realizing that Harry
Flowers had not bothered to introduce himself, assuming
Buddy would know who he was. Buddy said no more,
shrugging, unwilling to share family secrets with Harry
Flowers.

"You need action," Harry said, smiling his confident
and confidential smile. "A bit of diversion. A bit of
fun . . ." Waggling his fingers, eyebrows dancing. Aston-
ishing: cool Harry Flowers doing a Groucho imitation.

Buddy did not discover booze that first night with
Harry. But he discovered the marvelous escape it provided.
He had taken drinks before at parties or quick gulps from
a pint bottle in a paper bag at football games. The excitement of drinking had intoxicated him more than the liquor
itself. Or what he regarded as intoxication. But sitting in
the front seat of the car with Harry while Randy Pierce and
Marty Sanders carried on their Abbott and Costello routines in the backseat, Buddy discovered the marvelous
methods of booze, the way it soothed and stroked, made
hazy the harshness of things, made him—almost—happy.
Languid, and feeling what the hell.

That first night, they only drank and talked and joked
and Harry dropped him off in front of his house. Buddy
made his way haphazardly up the front walk, stumbled going into the house, lucky his mother and Addy were asleep.
Fell into bed, the splendid magic of the booze tumbling
him into the bliss of sleep.

Later, came "Funtime," Harry's label for the exploits,
stupid when sober but exciting and daring when drunk.
The evenings always began the same, drinking leisurely in
the car while talking casually, joking, listening to Marty
and Randy's conversational routines in the backseat.
Buddy noticed after a while that Harry did not drink much,
if at all, but encouraged Buddy and the others to do so,
supplying an endless amount of booze. Including the gin
that became Buddy's personal drink. He loved the beautiful exotic smell of the gin and what it did to him. Finally,
Harry would cry out: "Funtime." And off they'd go.

To the movies where they caused disruptions, laughing
too raucously at scenes that were not funny at all, spilling
food, particularly popcorn, all over the place, tearing wrappers off candy bars and sending them flying through the
air, guffawing, scuffling mildly, knowing that the ushers

were high school kids, most of them easily intimidated, not eager to notify the theater manager about the noise and distractions.

Other nights they merely cruised the streets, searching for mischief, Harry intimidating other drivers by driving too fast or too slow, cutting in, tailgating.

One weekend Harry obtained some fireworks in New Hampshire while on a trip there with his parents and showed off his display of lethal-looking bombs, an evil grin on his face. Off they went to the countryside, the outskirts of Wickburg, where they blew up mailboxes with the miniature bombs, delighting in the *whomp* of the explosion, giddy and laughing as they roared away. What made this especially exciting, Harry said, was that blowing up mailboxes was a federal offense.

Sometimes, their exploits were senseless, war-whooping their way through Jedson Park, disturbing couples making out in the dark, tossing debris into the decorative pots, pissing in fountains. The next morning, Buddy would shudder, recalling dimly the events of the night before. Those mornings presented him with his first hangovers—stomach in distress, eyes like raw wounds, head bulging with pain plus the knowledge that he had acted shamefully the night before. Looking at himself in the mirror, seeing the perspiring sallow flesh, the bloodshot eyes, the unkempt hair, he vowed that he would not allow Harry to lead him into further "Funtimes." But somehow by nightfall, he would capitulate again, following Harry Flowers wherever he went.

More than Harry, however, was the liquor that forgave everything. "Funtime" with Harry Flowers and the stooges gave him camaraderie, a sense of belonging to something. Drinking, however, gave him bliss in his loneliness. When he drank and began to drift, the lovely vagueness taking over his sensibilities, he did not need comrades or companions. Needed nobody. Especially did not need his mother and father.

Artie's screaming began two weeks after the vandalism. The first time it happened, Jane vaulted from her sleep, unsure of the sound, unable to identify it immediately as screaming. There was silence for a moment, and she heard a door close and then a shriek, this time muffled. Instantly and completely awake, she checked the digital clock on the bedside table: *2:11*.

When the screaming began again, she slid out of bed, went to the doorway and listened, shivering a bit in the chill of night. The sounds came from the bathroom across the hallway from her bedroom. More screaming, more shrieking, sheer terror in the sound, which set off a kind of terror in her own self.

The oak floor was cold beneath her feet as she paused near the bathroom. Silence within now. Then, whimpering, like a small animal trapped and crying. As she opened the door slightly, she recognized the soothing murmurs of her mother and father. Peeking in, she saw her father sitting on the edge of the bathtub holding Artie in his arms while her mother knelt on the floor, her arms encircling Artie, whose face was pressed into the folds of his father's pajamas.

Artie began to scream again, lifting his face away from his father's protection, his eyes open in terror. Then became mute, silent, but holding himself rigid.

Her mother looked up and saw Jane.

"A nightmare," she said.

But it was not a nightmare. It was sheer terror that Artie could not remember when he finally woke up after a few minutes.

The terror happened three nights in succession, Artie

screaming and sobbing, eyes wide with horror as if he were witnessing acts so horrible and obscene that his mind refused to acknowledge them. His eyes were always wide open as if he were awake. Crying out inconsolably, he inhabited a private world nobody else could enter, beyond the borders of comfort or consolation.

On the fourth day, they took Artie to Dr. Allison back in Monument, their old family doctor who had taken care of the family during all their illnesses.

Dr. Allison ran all sorts of tests in the small clinic he operated. The tests were negative. He said that preadolescent boys sometimes experienced night terrors of this sort. They passed with time.

"Does he think it's connected with the vandalism?" Jane later asked her father.

"Possibly," her father said, weariness in his voice. "Dr. Allison wants us to keep in touch. He said that it's easy to deal with what can be seen—fractures, sprains, cuts and bruises. Or symptoms—fever, high blood pressure and such. But it's difficult dealing with something that you can't see. He said that in other cases of this sort, time takes care of it."

Dr. Allison had been right. A few days passed before Artie's next nighttime terror. Then they stopped. "Let's hope forever," her mother said. Jane and her parents remained tense each evening as bedtime approached and Jane, tossing in bed, felt that a part of them remained awake during the night listening and waiting.

And Artie? He remained an enigma to Jane and maybe her parents, too.

He had always been the standard kid brother, similar to the brothers of all her friends. A tease, a pain in the neck sometimes, living in the private, mysterious world of boyhood, secretive, furtive, coming and going but barely touching her life except when he chose to torment her with his bathroom humor. His vocabulary was filled with words to describe bodily functions with which he plagued Jane when out of their parents' earshot. He also provided sound effects for those same functions, which drove Jane out of the house, hands over her ears.

"Is Artie okay?" Kenny Crane called to her one day from across the street while she was out half-jogging.

She pulled up. "I guess so," she said, puzzled at the concern on Kenny's thin face. She crossed over to him. "Why are you asking?"

Kenny lifted his thin shoulders in a kind of shrug. "I dunno," he said. "He doesn't hang out anymore. We used to swap Nintendos but now he's not interested."

"I think Artie's going through a bad time," Jane said. "Like everybody does once in a while. But he'll be all right." Telling him nothing, actually, because she herself did not know what was wrong with Artie.

"Artie's my friend," Kenny declared, chin lifted, his words sounding like a challenge.

After that brief talk with Kenny Crane, Jane kept track of Artie's comings and goings and discovered that he did not play his crazy video games anymore and, in fact, seldom went into his room except to change his clothes after school and go to bed. He wandered the neighborhood and sometimes disappeared for hours on his bike.

"Where do you go?" Jane asked when he returned from one of his trips and was tightening the bike chain.

"No place," he said.

This had always been his standard answer, even before the vandalism.

"You had to go *someplace*," she declared.

He shrugged, concentrating on the chain.

"How come you don't play your Nintendos anymore?"

she asked. Then, deciding to use a bit of flattery, "
thought you were an ace with the games." *Ace,* one of hi
words.

He shrugged again, looking away. "I kind of lost inter
est. It's kid stuff, anyway."

"Kid stuff? I thought you had to be some kind of ge
nius to play those games."

He looked directly at her, squinting: "How com
you're so interested, all of a sudden?"

"It's not the games I'm interested in, it's you. And wh
you're not playing them anymore. . . ."

No answer but at least he wasn't walking away fron
her. She took the big plunge. "Has it got something to d
with what happened to Karen? The vandalism?"

No answer again, still fiddling around with the bike.

"I don't like our house anymore," he said, speaking s
low that she barely heard the words. "I hate Burnside
too."

"I'm not crazy about it either," she said. "But we'v
got to live here. We just can't move."

"Why not? We moved here from Monument. Wh
can't we move again?"

"You heard what Dad said. That would be giving in
Artie." She saw him suddenly not as a bratty kid but as
troubled boy for whom she had a lot of affection.

"Giving in?" he asked, looking up at last. "To who?"

"To whoever did that to us," she said. "I think maybe
they'd like us to move, to show that they changed ou
lives." Discovering the thought for the first time as sh
spoke. "And damn it, Artie, we can't let them do that."

He grimaced, eyes narrowing.

"Can we?"

"I guess not," he said, looking directly at her.

She felt that for the first time they had somehow

touched each other as human beings. She had to stifle a desire to embrace him, the way she would embrace a friend.

"Think about it, okay?" she asked.

He nodded, their eyes meeting again before he went back to working on his bike. We connected, she thought, pleased, as she went into the house.

But Artie still did not play his video games.

Three weeks after Vaughn Masterson's funeral The Avenger's grandfather had begun asking him questions about his stolen gun.

"Know what's funny about that gun?"

"What's funny, Gramps?" The Avenger asked, keeping his face blank.

"Here's what's funny," said Gramps, who always talked slow and easy, drawing out his words. "I wonder how anybody from outside could have stolen my piece."

He always called his gun his *piece* but the word that hung in the air now, menacing and threatening, was *outside*.

The Avenger did not say anything. His grandfather liked to talk. The Avenger always let him ramble on. Most times, he was a good talker and told stories about his days on the police force, especially the old days when he walked the beat in the toughest section of town, where the wise guys hung around.

"I mean," his grandfather went on as if answering a question The Avenger had asked, "I always keep the doors locked. How did the thief get into the place? No visible signs of entry."

The Avenger swallowed. "Maybe he had a key."

"A key?" His grandfather turned and fastened his dark brown eyes on him, his policeman's eyes.

"Maybe one of those skeleton keys you told me about, the kind that fits all doors?" The Avenger said, gulping.

"Not this door, not this lock," his grandfather said. "This is a special police bolt. Nope, we have to rule out a key. What does that leave?"

His grandfather was still looking at him and The Avenger tried not to blink. "The windows?" he inquired. "You keep them open sometimes to catch a breeze."

"In two words: im-possible," his grandfather said. He was always quoting a man by the name of Sam Goldwyn, an old-time movie producer who said crazy things. Like: include me out. "How could anybody reach a fifth-floor window?"

"A ladder?" The Avenger ventured.

His grandfather did not bother to dignify the suggestion but snorted and looked out at the park, suddenly very interested in the joggers passing by. They were sitting on a bench in Cannon Park, across from the high school, basking in the September sun. Resting my bones, his grandfather called it. He had been a policeman for forty-five years, most of them standing on his dogs. He always called his feet *dogs*. He never drove a cruiser, always walked a beat. That's what's wrong with the world, he said, not enough cops on the sidewalks. Should take them out of the cruisers and put them on the sidewalks.

"If I didn't know any better, I would say it was an inside job," his grandfather said now, stretching his legs before him, folding his hands over his small round belly and closing his eyes.

The Avenger hoped he was about to take a nap, something his grandfather did at all hours of the day and night, slipping into sleep without any warning at all.

"What do you mean, inside job?" He was sorry he

asked the minute the words were out of his mouth because he had a good idea of what an *inside job* was.

"Means somebody inside the place stole the piece," his grandfather said. "Which is again im-possible. I'm the only one living here."

"A visitor maybe?" The Avenger said, grimacing. Why couldn't he keep his mouth shut?

"Not likely," he said, voice faint. He seemed to be drifting off, into his nap maybe. "I only got four rooms. The piece was hidden away in the closet. Bullets in a separate box. No way a visitor could sneak *two* boxes out. Unless . . ."

His voice grew even fainter and a moment later a soft snore came from his mouth, fluttering the ends of his mustache. The Avenger sighed "Whew . . ." softly, glad that the conversation was over. But he frowned as he stretched his own legs in front of him, although they barely touched the ground.

"Of course, my memory isn't what it used to be," his grandfather said, startling The Avenger, who thought he was sound asleep. His grandfather spoke without opening his eyes, his hands folded on his round stomach. "Maybe I *did* leave the door unlocked by mistake. Maybe somebody *did* get into the place." Silence for a while. "Can't trust anybody these days. Anybody . . ." His eyes were still closed.

Anybody.

The word echoed in his mind, the way *inside job* had echoed earlier.

He tried to finish the sentence that began with that word: Anybody . . . anybody in the world. Anybody . . . even you!

The Avenger leaped with alarm, as if his grandfather had actually said the words, had flung the accusation at him. But the old man was still napping, eyes closed, breath rattling through his partly opened mouth.

The Avenger closed his own eyes and made himself sit still on the bench, even though his nose immediately began to itch. He did not scratch it. He did not move at all, not even his eyelids. He sat there thinking *anybody* until his grandfather woke up, snorting and coughing. They walked out of the park in silence.

The silence lasted all the way home and was worse even than that word *anybody*. His grandfather did not tousle his hair and pat his head as he usually did when he said good-bye to The Avenger at the corner of Spruce and Elm.

The telephone rang as Buddy came into the house from school. Dumping his books on the couch in the family room, he picked up the receiver. Then was sorry he'd answered. Harry was on the line.

"Want some fun tonight, Buddee?"

That cool insinuating voice, this time a French accent.

"Not tonight," Buddy answered, clearing his throat first to make his voice steady. Feeling guilty about the house they vandalized, he had promised himself that he wouldn't take part in any more of Harry's adventures. Drinking was one thing, the exploits were another.

"Busee? Beeg plans? Too beeg for your friends?" Maybe he was trying a Mexican accent.

"No, it's not that," Buddy said, mind racing to find an excuse and coming up blank. Except for: "I've got a lot of homework tonight." Frowning, knowing how lame this sounded.

Silence from Harry's end of the line. A silence filled with disbelief, Buddy knew. Then: "Conscience bothering you, Buddy?" In his normal voice.

That was Harry, always capable of coming at you from

your blind side. "Not really," Buddy said, grimacing. "I'm just not in the mood." Then, loading his voice with sincerity: "And I do have an awful lot of homework." Somebody once said that if you can learn to fake sincerity, you'll be a success in life.

"Plan on drinking alone?"

"What?"

"That's a sure sign, Buddy."

"Sure sign of what?" Buddy, helpless, asked. Not wanting to ask, not wanting to continue this conversation but helpless to end it.

"Alcoholism. Drinking alone is one of the sure signs."

"I'm not going to drink," Buddy replied. "Alone or otherwise." But he was going to do exactly that.

That was one of the reasons why he disliked Harry Flowers so much: He always spoiled things. What was wrong with a drink now and then? Or whether he drank alone or not? Harry delighted in finding the rotten side of anything. Always lifting a lid to reveal something terrible underneath. Like the other day in the park.

He and Harry had been sitting in the car, trying to figure out what to do for "Funtime" that night, although Buddy hoped that they wouldn't do anything, still recoiling from the events at the house they'd wrecked.

Children frolicked in the park, soaring high on the swings, swooping down the slides, the air filled with happy squeals and laughter. Some little girls held hands as they walked around in a circle singing:

"Ring around the rosy . . . a pocket full of posies . . . ashes, ashes . . . we all fall down . . ."

"Stupid," Harry said.

"What's stupid?" Buddy asked, annoyed that Harry would find something stupid about a bunch of kids playing in a park.

"Those little girls don't know what they're doing," Harry said, pointing with his chin. "Potter in English Lit. last week told us all about this nursery rhyme. It's what kids sang back in the olden days when the Black Plague was killing millions of people. People would get a rosy kind of rash and rubbed themselves with herbs and posies. Then they fell down and died. . . ."

Buddy scowled, kept his eyes on the little girls, who had scrambled to their feet again, preparing to form another circle.

"Know what you are, Harry?" he asked. "You're a spoiler. I always thought Ring-Around-the-Rosy was kind of a nice thing for kids to do. But now you've gone and spoiled it all."

"I'm sorry, Buddy, but I didn't make up that story," Harry said. He did not sound sorry. "I aced the test Potter gave and that's why I remember it at all. I usually don't go in for that nursery rhyme kind of crap."

"It's not crap," Buddy said as the little girls began to circle, singing the song again, their small voices rising in the air.

"Ashes, ashes . . ."

One little girl with long blond hair tripped and stumbled.

"We all fall down . . ."

Down they went on the grass, in a tumble of arms and legs, the blond girl crying, her cheeks shiny with tears.

"Maybe it isn't crap, after all," Harry said. "Because we all fall down, don't we?" His voice dry, sharp as ice cubes clinking.

And on the telephone now, his voice was dry and icy again as he said: "Of course you're not going to drink alone."

Then snapping words like whips: "Remember this,

Buddy. What happened the other night, you enjoyed it. You got your kicks. You're probably having conscience trouble now, but you had fun that night."

Buddy didn't answer. And didn't try to deny it. Because Harry was right, damn it. Buddy *had* enjoyed himself, found great satisfaction smashing and trashing that house, like striking back at his mother and father and the whole goddam world. Or was that only an excuse? But an excuse for what?

"Right, Buddy?" That cool persistent voice.

"Right, Harry," Buddy said, capitulating. *But I didn't pee against the wall. And I didn't attack the girl.*

"Good, Buddy. Which means you're one of us."

But I didn't help the girl, either, did I? Did not come to her rescue like a hero. Some hero, Buddy.

"See, Buddy? You're not alone. You don't have to drink alone."

Buddy let a sigh escape his lips. Then tried to inject his voice with more of the old sincerity.

"I know that, Harry, and I appreciate it. But, actually, I *do* have all this stupid homework and I don't feel that great. Maybe it's the flu bug or something . . ."

"Sure, Buddy. I was just checking in, anyway." Brief pause. "Take it easy, Buddee." French again. "Zee you around . . ."

And hung up before Buddy could answer.

Jane's visits to the hospital had become as much a routine part of her life as going to school. Although Karen did not respond during Jane's visits, she felt a closeness to her she had never known before. Sometimes she held her hand, placed her finger on Karen's wrist and was gratified to feel the pulse throbbing regularly, strong and vital. She pretended the pulse was a kind of Morse code by which

Karen was telling her that she would come back, don't worry, all will turn out fine.

Occasionally, when nurses had to attend to Karen's needs, Jane wandered the hospital corridors, trying not to look into the rooms she passed, not wanting to observe other people's misery or to invade their privacy. One afternoon, she discovered the hospital chapel. Barely a chapel, nondenominational, pews without kneelers, subdued lighting, a faked stained-glass window, back lit, set into the inner wall. Sitting in the pew, removed from all the activity outside the door, she discovered a kind of serenity. She even prayed, sort of, altering the old prayers of her childhood for Karen . . . "God is great, God is good, please help Karen to get better . . ." and "Now I sit me down to rest, I pray for God to help my sister." . . . Should have felt silly doing such a thing, silly and irreverent, but didn't.

She realized that she had not really prayed for a very long time. Although she and her family attended Sunday services regularly, Karen had simply gone through the motions. Sunday mornings at the old Methodist church back in Monument had been more of a social act than religious. She liked to see the families gathering in the churchyard after services. Pastor William Smith had been old and holy and devout but also immensely boring. Here in Burnside, her parents had enrolled the family in the local Methodist church, a building so modern it resembled a recreation center, and the pews arranged in the round, like in a theater. The pastor here was not old or boring but he tried too hard, preached too long, and Jane's mind wandered. Why do we go to church, anyway? she wondered. Somehow she believed—and did not know where that belief came from —that if you were kind and patient and did not hurt anyone intentionally, you would go to heaven someday. *Someday* seemed so far away that she did not think about it often. But she thought about it now in the chapel. I must make myself a better person, she vowed. Ran through the Ten Commandments, those she could remember, shocked to find she could only think of two or three—Thou shalt not steal, thou shalt not kill, thou shalt not covet. She did not steal or kill or covet, dimly aware that *covet* meant being envious. But what was that to brag about? Honor thy father and mother. I must do better by my mother and father, she thought. Must be kinder to them, help them get over this. But didn't know how.

In the hospital chapel, she realized she had not been aware of that terrible smell for a few days. Had it gone forever?

Returning from the chapel one day, she heard her mother talking to Karen as she turned to enter the room. Hoping that Karen could hear them, the family kept her up-to-date on what was going on at home, and in the neighborhood. Her friends from school reported almost daily, hesitant at first, but quickly losing their self-consciousness as they told her what was happening at Burnside High.

Arrested by the anguish in her mother's voice, Jane found herself shamelessly eavesdropping.

"I don't know what to do. I shouldn't be saying this to you but I've got to talk to someone. I have this crazy thought, Karen, that something is holding you back from regaining consciousness. Because you're afraid. Of something. Don't be. Don't be afraid. We all love you. We'll protect you. That terrible vandalism won't happen again. We've had a real good alarm system installed. We'll take care of you . . ."

Silence now in the room. No response from Karen, of course. Peering in, she saw Karen, eyes closed, silent in the bed. The anguish—more like desperation—in her mother's voice caused Jane to draw back. She did not want to confront her mother at this moment. Her mother had been putting on such a show of bravery as she cheerfully went about her housework, her daily errands. All of it a sham. Pretending for the sake of the family.

"You've got to come back, Karen. Until you do, nothing will be right. We all live in the same house but we are separate. We aren't a family anymore."

Which was true, Jane admitted with a kind of horror. They were all so polite with each other. *Pass the salt, please. That's a pretty blouse, Jane. Wonderful report card, Artie.* Not like the old days of family arguments about staying out late, mediocre report cards, who's wearing whose sweater. Now they treated each other as if they were made of glass, would shatter if a cross word was uttered.

Jane did not finally enter the room, left her mother to carry on that sad one-sided conversation, and returned to the chapel, instead.

Buddy opened the letter which wasn't really a letter at all, not tearing the envelope but slitting it open carefully with a kitchen knife. Doing it slowly, which allowed him time to ponder the possible contents. He knew what the *actual* contents would be—the weekly check his father sent him. Twenty-five dollars. Which was almost twice as much as his previous allowance when his father was still living at home. There was never anything else in the envelope and Buddy always pretended he wasn't disappointed. Screw it, he would mutter, crumpling the envelope and tossing it away. *Screw it all, Buddy, and cash the check.*

What he hoped for every week was a note from his father accompanying the check. He'd have been satisfied with a few words scrawled hastily on a scrap of paper. But the envelope always contained only the money. The twenty-five dollars was terrific, of course. That's what kept him supplied with booze. But—but what? He wasn't sure what.

His father had made no promises the day he left the house. He'd been in a hurry, hastily packing his clothes, frowning, scratching himself as if the clothes he wore were too tight for his body. He kept saying: *Sorry. Really sorry to be doing this to you, Buddy.* Throwing shirts every which way into his suitcase, sloppy to the end. *Tell Addy how sorry I am.* Addy had refused to speak to him, wouldn't open her bedroom door to him. *I'll send you your allowance every week—sorry it has to be by mail.* Sorry, sorry, sorry.

"Can't we get together sometime?" Buddy had asked.

"Sure, sure," his father replied, concentrating on the packing. That didn't sound at all convincing, sounded more like *no, no.* Watching his father struggling to close the bulging suitcase, Buddy realized that you could live all your life in the same house with a person and not really know him. His father had always been his Father. With a capital *F.* Did all the things a father was supposed to do. Went off to work and came home. Threw a baseball to Buddy in the backyard. Took him and Addy to the circus, to fireworks on the Fourth of July. Famous for naps, could drop off to sleep at the blink of an eye. Hated driving, let their mother drive on long trips while he dozed. *My sleepytime guy,* Buddy's mother called him affectionately, tenderly.

No more tenderness these days. His mother abandoned and the twenty-five-dollar check in the mail. That's what his father had become.

Twice he had called his father at the office. More *sorry*s. *Too busy. Maybe next week. I'll call you.* He didn't call Buddy but the checks still came. The checks which bought the booze and the booze which made it easier not to have his father get in touch.

Now, he looked at another check, looked at the signature he had seen on report cards until recently. His mother had signed his report card last week. In a sudden fury, he thought: I should send this check back, show him that he can't buy me off with money.

He found an envelope in his mother's desk in the den, along with a ballpoint pen. Wrote his father's name on the envelope, his address at the office. Tore a sheet of paper from the pad his mother kept on hand for making notes. Pondered what he should say. Decided he would not say anything. Let the returned check speak for him. He found a small book of stamps in the drawer, detached one and placed it on the envelope. Slipped the check, folded over once, inside. Licked the flap, sealed the envelope, sighed with relief. *It was better to do something than do nothing.* Some writer had once said that.

He checked his wallet—three lonely one-dollar bills. Buying liquor at his age was not only illegal but also expensive. Harry had introduced him to a homeless downtown wanderer called Crumbs, unshaven, bleary-eyed, pushing a grocery cart filled with rags and paper bags whose contents Buddy could only guess at. Despite his name and his slovenly appearance, Crumbs was a shrewd businessman. He charged a flat rate of five dollars a bottle for his services, which did not include the price of the booze itself. Even if Buddy ordered only a pint, which carried a price tag of less than four dollars, the service charge did not change. This often forced Buddy to order a quart bottle.

As a result, he had come to rely on his father's extra twenty-five-dollar allowance. With the addition of the fifteen-dollar allowance from his mother, the total should have been more than sufficient. But wasn't. He also had to pay for everyday expenses out of that sum, plus lunches at school and the extra money spent when he was out with Harry and the stooges.

For the next two days, he carried the envelope with the check inside his jacket pocket. Approached several mailboxes, checked the pick-up times on the inside of the cover as he balanced the envelope in his hand. Finally, he did not mail the check. Why should his father get away without paying for his freedom? Why shouldn't he pay, even a little bit, for what he had done? Twenty-five dollars was cheap enough. A bargain.

The Avenger was amazed to find out how easy it was to commit murder twice and get away with it. He learned something new each time. First, he had learned about the importance of motive—or lack of it—when he killed Vaughn Masterson. What he learned the second time was that you did not need a weapon, like a gun or a knife, to kill someone. Of course, you needed opportunity. And sometimes you had to wait for the opportunity. Or, as in the case of the second time, the opportunity presented itself when you weren't even sure you wanted to commit murder. That was another lesson he learned: Be on your toes, be alert all the time, ready to take advantage of any opportunity that might come up.

The way it had happened with his grandfather.

He had not planned to kill his grandfather that Saturday afternoon. He had, in fact, been avoiding him, afraid to hear more questions about the gun. His grandfather visited The Avenger and his mother once or twice a week because he knew she was often lonesome. The Avenger's father had left town a long time ago, without saying goodbye or leaving a note. His mother did not believe that he had abandoned them or met with foul play or had been killed in an accident. She believed he had somehow lost his memory.

She pictured him—and so did The Avenger—roaming the world, trying to find his way home. His picture sat on the television set and his father's face was burned into The Avenger's mind. He searched every day for his father, studying the faces of all the men he met on the street. He hadn't found him yet.

When his grandfather visited, he brought good stuff to eat and sometimes flowers for his mother. He called The Avenger's mother "daughter," although she was not his daughter. They sat and watched television, all the soap operas, and later they shut off the set and his grandfather would talk about the old days, his days on the beat or about when "Donnie," The Avenger's father, was a boy.

"Don't see much of you these days, keed," his grandfather said the last time he visited. He often called him "keed."

"I've been busy," The Avenger said, his face growing warm. "School, helping out Mom." Which was true. The Avenger always helped out his mother. Did the daily chores without being told. Ran the errands. These days, when his grandfather visited, he made himself scarce, sometimes left the house before the old man arrived or got out of the place as soon as possible.

"You make me feel bad, keed," his grandfather said, "running off all the time." And for an instant he felt bad for the old man, realized that he looked *really* old these days, frail and skinny.

"Sorry, Gramps," he said. And he *was* sorry. Sorry for the circumstances that made his grandfather an enemy, somebody to be suspicious of.

"He's such a good boy," his mother said, in her wispy voice. "He takes such good care of me . . ."

"I know, Ella, I know," his grandfather said, his voice soft and gentle. But his eyes weren't gentle. When The Avenger looked up at the old man's eyes, they were shrewd and glittering. They studied him, bore down into him. The Avenger always looked away.

The next week when he answered the telephone, his grandfather's voice greeted him: "Hi, keed, how's tricks?"

What did he mean by *tricks*?

"Fine, Gramps," he said, keeping his voice bright, determined to be natural.

"Listen, this is an invitation to go out with your old Gramps. You're so busy these days I figure I got to make a formal invitation. So—how about next Saturday afternoon?"

The Avenger swallowed hard, felt his Adam's apple bouncing up and down. "Well . . ." His mind raced, looking for an excuse. Trying at the same time to gauge his grandfather's voice, looking for secret things in the voice.

"I figure we can go to the movies. There's a good cop movie coming up next week." They both liked cop movies with gunfire and car chases and explosions. "Then we can grab some grub." He always called the hamburgers at McDonald's "grub." "What say?"

What could he say? He had to say yes. He did not want to spend any time at all with Gramps but the movie theater was the best place of all if he had to do it.

As it turned out, they had a good time at the movies. Loaded up with popcorn and M&Ms and Cokes and enjoyed all the action on the screen, especially the long chase across streets and bridges between a car and a *man*, a policeman.

They were both too full of candy and junk to grab some grub at McDonald's but instead walked leisurely along to his grandfather's apartment. "For a good talk," his grandfather said, which made the day turn cloudy although the sun was warm on his cheeks.

His grandfather's apartment was small and cramped. The Avenger found himself out of breath, as if the walls were closing in on him. The apartment was in a high-rise for the elderly. What they called a four-room living area, although it was actually three rooms, the dining room and kitchen combined in one room. The only thing The Avenger liked about the apartment was the balcony, with iron railings, five stories high, looking out over the town. You could see across the smaller buildings to the hills in the distance. Sometimes, his grandfather brought out his binoculars and The Avenger studied the windows of the other buildings or looked down at the people walking below.

"Want some Coke?" his grandfather asked.

The Avenger shook his head. "No thanks, Gramps."

"Cookies? Piece of cake?"

"Still full, Gramps."

What he wanted was to go home. His eyes ached a bit and his head hurt.

"Feeling all right?" his grandfather asked, eyes narrowed as he studied The Avenger.

"Ate too much," The Avenger said. He was afraid he was going to be sick. He felt hot all over, not warm but hot.

"Let's get some fresh air," his grandfather said, heading for the small balcony. "We can talk better out there. We can sit and talk."

But his grandfather did not sit. He told The Avenger to sit down in the black wrought-iron chair but he himself leaned against the railing, his back to the town, his eyes on The Avenger. He began to ask questions. About school. How were his marks? Was his spelling improving? What did he do after school besides the chores? Stuff like that.

The Avenger answered the questions willingly, talking fast, going into details, simply to hold off more questions. He had a feeling his grandfather was not really listening to the answers, his eyes kind of glazed now, as if he was seeing things far away or thinking of something else altogether.

Finally, the old man turned his back on The Avenger. Leaned against the balcony railing, looked out over the city. "I've got to ask you something important, keed," he said, his voice muffled a bit.

Important. The word made The Avenger's insides shrivel.

He knew the question: Did you kill Vaughn Masterson?

That's why his grandfather could not face him. He was like the district attorney in the TV movies who turned away from the killer in the witness stand and faced the jury to ask his questions. Like the whole city out there was now the jury and he, The Avenger, was on the witness stand.

The Avenger had to say something. So he said: "What do you want to ask me, Gramps?" Keeping his voice bright as usual.

Then the moment arrived.

As if it had been planned that way.

"Hey, what's that?" his grandfather asked, distracted, leaning forward over the railing, checking something down below.

The Avenger began to get up from his chair and suddenly everything was in slow motion, which was crazy because he was moving very fast, his arms and legs working perfectly, beautifully, as he leaped up but also slow, slow as possible, moving across the balcony, as if he were off somewhere watching himself running now, fast, hands raised in front of him, as his grandfather began to turn almost as if he had heard an alarm going off and was half turned when

The Avenger, no longer watching now but *doing it,* crashed into him. Crashed into him low, not slow motion either but fast, fast, and low, just below his behind, the thin hard bones there, and lifting at the same time, finding somehow the strength, the determination, the *means* to do it, and desperate, too, because he knew that he could not fail, it would be the end of everything if he failed. Without warning, his grandfather seemed to lift himself up, his hands flung out, and he was propelled upward as if he were about to fly, his long thin arms like the wings of an airplane or a wounded bird and he wailed, a terrible sound coming out of him, as he was caught and held for one moment in the air, arms flailing, grabbing nothing. Then he fell. Like a puppet whose strings were cut, like a tree branch taken by the wind. Down he went, all arms and legs thrashing the air.

At the last moment, The Avenger took his eyes away from his grandfather's downward flight. Did not want to see him land on the pavement below. Like in the movie when the camera turned away at the last minute and you gave a big sigh of relief because you did not want to see the smashing, the splatter, all of that.

He withdrew from the railings and sat in the chair for a moment. Waited to hear something. But did not hear anything. Did not hear screams or sirens or anything. As if he had gone deaf. He counted to ten. Slowly. Then he went into the apartment and picked up the telephone, paused a moment, and remembering the instructions about emergencies he had learned at school, he punched 911 and told whoever answered to please send an ambulance, his poor old Gramps had fallen off his balcony.

Jane woke up with a start, having heard *something*—a footstep in the hallway? a door closing?—and wondered if somehow the trashers had come back, had broken into the house in the middle of the night. Then calmed down as she recognized her father's footsteps as he padded down the hallway in his slippers on his way to the bathroom.

Unable to go back to sleep, she fought the blankets that seemed too heavy for this mild night. When she threw them off, her shoulders in the thin nylon nightgown grew cold. She thought of Karen in the hospital who slept night and day, did not know heat or cold. Realizing finally that her father had not returned from the bathroom, she sat up in bed, saw the time in the glowing red figures of the digital clock: 2:57.

She slipped out of bed, went down the hallway, saw, at the head of the stairs, a spill of light below. She found her father in the kitchen, leaning against the sink, a glass of milk in his hand.

"What's the matter, Dad?"

"Couldn't sleep," he said, yawning, but a fake yawn, rubbing his hand across his faint stubble of beard.

"You always sleep like the proverbial log," she said, quoting his own words.

He smiled, a small wan smile. "Things change," he said. "Somebody said your body changes completely every seven years. Maybe I'm going into a new cycle."

Which she did not for a minute believe.

Studying him surreptitiously, she realized that people do not often look at each other. Not even fathers. Her father had grown a mustache a few years ago, wore it for a few months and then shaved it off one morning before breakfast. No one at the breakfast table noticed his clean-shaven upper lip. When he was leaving the house to go to work, Artie, whose sharp eyes missed very little, said: "Hey, Dad, something wrong with your face?" But even Artie had not realized the mustache was gone, only that their father's face looked different that day. Her mother finally noticed the missing mustache at the dinner table that night.

No missing mustache now, only her father looking forlorn and lonely at three in the morning. Hair disheveled, eyes dull, listless. Needing a shave. A faintly familiar tone to his voice when he spoke, disturbing to her. Where had she heard that voice before? Then remembered. The voice in which he answered the detective who had asked if he had any enemies. A small boy's voice. Not really her father. Jane got the shivers again as she had that day but worse now. Middle-of-the-night worse. She shivered, not from the cold, but from a sense of dread. She remembered a poem from school: "Things fall apart, the center cannot hold." Her family falling apart and her father, at the center. Could he hold them together? If he couldn't, who could?

"How about you, Jane? What are you doing up at this crazy hour?"

"I heard you come downstairs and wondered if you were okay, not sick or anything."

"I'm okay," he said. "Just restless."

Her father startled her with his next words.

"Actually, I had a bad dream," he said. "I've been having bad dreams lately. At least, I think they're bad dreams. They wake me up and I'm in a sweat but I can't remember the dreams, only the feeling of them, their aura. Like a black cloud, although the dreams aren't about black clouds. Just a feeling of something dark and menacing . . ."

Oh, Dad, don't say that. Fathers aren't supposed to have dreams like that. Kids run to their fathers in the middle of the night when the *kids* have bad dreams. Fathers are supposed to soothe them and say: It's only a dream, only a dream.

"Do you think the dream is about Karen? Because she's in kind of a black cloud?"

He glanced at her sharply.

"You think so?"

She shrugged. Tried to appear calm although panic whistled through her veins. He was supposed to know the answers.

"I worry about her, of course," he said. "We all do. I guess what's especially bad is the sense of helplessness. We can't do anything to help her . . ."

"Maybe she knows, Dad," Jane offered. "Maybe she *does* hear us when we visit and talk to her, like the doctor says. Knows we're there." She wasn't sure she believed this but needed to offer him comfort of some kind.

Silence for a while. Nighttime silence different from morning or afternoon. No cars passing, no shouts from kids outside. No lawn mowers. Not even the sounds of nature, birds, dogs, or cats.

Her father's jaw tightened, a pulse throbbing at his temples, lips pressed tight. "Another thing," he said, and the simmering anger again. "Helpless against who did this thing to her, to us. If I could get my hands on them . . ." He looked up at her sheepishly. "Sorry," he said. "This is middle-of-the-night talk, that's all." Rousing himself, pushing himself up from the table. "Let's go to bed, Jane. Sleep, the best medicine . . ."

Jane did not fall asleep for a long time. Tossed and turned. Got all mixed up between sheet and blankets. Punched the pillow. Could not get comfortable. Remembering that look on her father's face. The anger below the surface. The helplessness as he clenched his jaw. *If I could get my hands on them.*

She was suddenly afraid *for* her father.

And almost hoped that the trashers would never be found.

Buddy reached into the pile of rags, probing for the familiar touch of the paper bag and the bottle it contained. Felt—nothing. He groped further, to the left and right, mildly puzzled but not really concerned. Frowning, he cleared the shelf of the accumulation of rags, tools, old paint cans, placing them on the floor next to the workbench. Still not there. He looked under the shelf, scanned the floor. Even checked the old tin wastebasket next to the bench and the hanging shelf above the bench. No bag and no bottle.

Breathing a bit heavily, perspiration bubbling on his forehead, he leaned against the wall, eyes closed. He had heard that one of the bad effects of drinking was blackout. Had he somehow blacked out and couldn't remember where he'd placed the bottle? Ridiculous. His memory was sometimes hazy the day after a wild night but he had never drawn a blank.

"This what you're looking for?"

Turning, he saw Addy in the doorway, holding the bottle, her nose wrinkled as if a foul odor came from it.

"What the hell do you think you're doing?" Buddy asked, holding back an impulse to grab the bottle out of her hands.

"I'm trying to save your life."

"Save your own life," he said, walking toward her reaching out for the bottle.

She stepped back, moving the bottle away from him.

"*My* life's not in danger," she said. "I'm not in danger of becoming an alcoholic."

Buddy shook his head in disgust. "Look, there are

plenty of other bottles I can put my hands on," he said. "Keep the goddam thing. Have a drink or two yourself. Maybe it'll make you more human."

"Is that what you think it does? Make you more human? Let me tell you something Buddy. It does just the opposite. Makes you a monster. A silly-looking monster. Ever look into the mirror when you're so stupidly drunk? You ought to see yourself. That silly look on your face, like a moron. And you ought to see yourself at the dinner table. That stupid grin of yours. Mom won't admit it. She's so wrapped up in her own worries that she doesn't see *anything,* not even how stupid you look and act."

Silly, stupid. Didn't she know any other words?

"So you think you can stop me from being stupid and silly by taking my bottles?"

"Now you're being stupid and silly when you're sober. Bad enough when you're drunk but absolutely ridiculous when you're sober. I assume you're sober, anyway. So, no, I don't think taking this bottle will stop you from drinking."

"So what's this all about?"

"I'm simply trying to get your attention."

"Why do you need my attention? I don't need yours. Don't want yours."

"Because . . ." Now she faltered and the bottle in her hand seemed ludicrous.

"Because why?" Challenging her. *Okay, here I am, you have my attention. Now tell me why you need it.*

"Because we have to talk. I can't stand this any longer. Mom going around in a permanent daze, like she's sleepwalking. You drunk most of the time. Your father out there with that woman, that *girl.*"

"Well, what are we supposed to do?" he asked, but not really interested because there was nothing they could do.

Which, he decided, he ought to tell her: "There is nothing we can do."

She heaved the bottle as if throwing a football and it struck the stucco wall, breaking into a thousand pieces, the neck flying away while the rest of the bottle and the precious liquid dropped to the floor.

"Christ," he said.

"See? There's always something that can be done."

"And you think you've been acting like a sane person?"

Which made it a draw, as he turned to look at the soggy mess on the floor.

"Look," she said, conciliatory. "All I want to do is talk. Is that asking too much? And I've got a present for you. In my room." She took a step toward the hallway. "Please," she said, her voice cracking forlornly.

Reluctant but curious he followed as she led him upstairs to her room, opened the door and gestured him inside. She pointed to the bureau where a gleaming bottle of gin stood, a glass beside it.

"Help yourself," she said. "From me to you."

His first reaction was to think that Addy was a boozer, too, with her own secrets but a moment later realized that this was not possible. Not Addy, of all people.

"No, the bottle's not mine," she said. "I wouldn't drink this stuff for anything in the world. And never mind how I got it. It involved bribes, from the friend of a friend. But I got it for you and this is another bribe. So that we'd talk. If you have to drink, then do it with me. Not alone. I can't stand being alone in this house anymore."

Suddenly, he did not want a drink. His eyes became ridiculously wet and he fumbled in his pocket for a stray piece of Kleenex. Saw how pathetic they'd become, brother and sister: the brother a drunk, the sister abandoned, tracking down a bottle of gin in order to make contact.

"We've got to do something, Buddy," she said. "We can't keep on like this. Remember the sins of omission?"

Buddy shook his head, didn't remember. He remembered only vaguely those religion classes on Monday nights in the basement of St. Dymphna's church. Old Father O'Brien conducted the classes, explaining the Bible and the Ten Commandments and other stuff. Buddy had paid scant attention. Monday nights were ridiculous nights for religion classes. Kids were already loaded up with regular homework. His mother insisted that he and Addy attend the classes. "Her conscience bothering her," Addy surmised. Their mother was Roman Catholic and their father a Presbyterian if he was anything at all. He seldom bothered going to church. Their mother herded them to Sunday masses and Christian Doctrine classes on Monday evenings. Until the last two or three years when she seemed to give up on the classes although she made Buddy and Addy sit through interminable services on Sunday morning, or sometimes Saturday evenings. Saturday evenings were even worse than Sunday mornings.

"The sins of omission are the sins of doing nothing," Addy said now in her smart-alecky way. "Like, I think wars get declared because somebody somewhere does nothing to stop them. And we're doing nothing to stop what's going on with Mom and Dad."

"But what can we do?" he asked, still not looking at her, his eyes remaining moist, concentrating on the window and the yellow plastic butterfly she'd installed to cover a hole in the screen.

"I don't know. But let's talk about it. About the possibilities."

Which made him realize that Addy dreamed of possibilities when she was sober and he only indulged in them when he was on the booze. "Okay, let's talk . . ."

"Do you need a drink first?" she asked.

The word *need* stung him, made him flinch. Was she being sarcastic? Saw her face and decided she was sincere.

"No," he said, glad to be saying no. "Let's hear about these possibilities."

Addy flung herself on the bed, cupped hands holding her chin, while Buddy went to the window, stared at the backyard where the old picnic table needed paint and the barbecue grill rusted away. The family suppers out there were only dim memories now.

"Maybe," Addy said, "we ought to have plans."

"What kind of plans?" Speaking almost absently, still staring into the yard.

"Plans to end this crazy stuff between Mom and Dad. Maybe we can do something to get them together again. At least to talk . . ." She launched into a series of plots—arranging a meeting between them on "neutral ground," like in a restaurant. Approaching that woman, *that girl,* as Addy always described her scornfully, and trying to reason with her. "If she sees us, his son and daughter, she probably will *see him* in a different light."

All of it impossible, of course. Which he tried to tell her without hurting her feelings or fracturing this sudden intimacy. "Addy, this is dream stuff. Sounds beautiful but I don't think it can work. That woman, that girl—you can bet your life she's already seen us, she knows who we are. And getting Mom and Dad together—do you think that can really work out? This thing just didn't happen overnight. Who knows when it began? Maybe Mom and Dad began falling apart long before that woman came along. . . ."

"Maybe we could sue them," she said, brightly, the kind of brightness that flashes just before tears.

They both laughed, brittle laughter ringing hollowly in the bedroom and as they looked at each other Buddy saw that they had accomplished something, at least, a sort of bond, not exactly friendship but a kind of alliance.

"Know what we are, Buddy?" Addy asked, voice rueful.

"What?" Buddy replied warily, a bit unsure of himself with this new Addy.

"Victims. Victims of child abuse."

"Wait a minute," he said. "Mom and Dad never laid a hand on us." Frowning, suddenly aghast: "Did something happen to you? Did Dad ever . . ."

"That's not what I mean," she scoffed, and for a moment she was the old Addy again, the pain-in-the-ass kid sister. "Not sexual abuse or even physical abuse. But just as bad in its own way. Divorce. A family breaking up. Mothers and fathers too selfish about themselves and ignoring their children . . ."

"They haven't ignored us," Buddy said, not certain why he was defending them. "Mom's here. Dad keeps in touch." That twenty-five-dollar check each week.

"That's not what I mean by ignoring. I mean, ignoring the hurt, the invisible stuff that happens to kids. What's happening to us."

Buddy hated arguments, confrontations, did not like to articulate feelings, as if feelings would go away or would not have any existence at all if they were not put into words. He did not comment. In fact, he wanted to end this conversation, get out of here.

"Listen, Buddy, when I fell out of the tree that time I was nine years old and broke my arm, I didn't cry. It hurt like hell but I didn't cry. But I've cried three times since Dad left. Middle-of-the-night crying."

Tears gathered now in her eyes and she turned away smacking her hands together the way a pitcher does before throwing the ball to a batter. His little sister in this pathetic parody of a ball player simply because she was trying to hide her tears.

"I hate them, I hate them," she muttered, still turned away, still smacking her hands together.

He looked at the bottle on the bureau, the glass beside it. Reached out to touch her shoulder but unable, again, to do it. Reached out toward the bottle but stayed his hand

"Don't hate them, Addy," he said. "Anyway, Mom's still here. Dad was the one who left."

"But he wouldn't have left, wouldn't have been attracted to someone else if everything had been fine with them." Turning to him again: "Why doesn't she fight back?"

That's the difference between us, Buddy thought. Addy was a fighter, his mother wasn't. Neither was he. He drifted, let others do the leading. Like with Harry Flowers Following him in his exploits, into that house and the terrible things they did. "I don't know," he said, feeling useless

"Poor Buddy." Almost whispering, her voice sad and wistful.

He went to the door, unable to say any more. He did not want her pity. Did not want her bottle. Did not completely trust her yet. Maybe later. All he knew now was that he wanted to get out of the house, wanted to get downtown where Crumbs would supply him with the stuff that would take away all the lousy things in his life.

The Avenger hated the Mall.
He hated the crowds and the white lights and the mu-

sic coming from the loudspeakers. He felt lost and alone, not like an Avenger at all, his head aching from all the sights and sounds, his eyes sore from all the searching and looking. He was surprised to find so many old people in the Mall, looking sad and abandoned, lingering on the benches, some of them staring into space, others napping, eyes closed, mouths open.

The teenagers were everywhere. Moving, always on the go. Alone and in groups. Laughing and calling to each other. The guys pushing and shoving sometimes. Flirting with the girls and the girls flirting back, sidelong glances, secret smiles. Eating hot dogs and pizzas and big crazy sandwiches. Gulping Coke, 7-Up, other stuff.

Although he hated the Mall, he went there every day when the schools let out, having decided, through a process of elimination, that the Mall was the most likely place to find the trashers. He had reached this conclusion one day in his shed, where he had put his thinking cap on. Whenever he came across a tough problem, his mother always said: Put your thinking cap on. So that's what he did. In his mind, he made out a list. He was good at picturing things in his mind. On one side, he saw the questions. On the other side, the answers. Like: What do you know about the trashers? Answer: They are young guys, all dressed up, teenagers. To find them you have to go where teenagers hang out, right? Right. And where do teenagers hang out? At the schools, high schools. Do teenagers really hang out at schools? Don't they get out of the schools as fast as possible when the last bell rings? Right. Where do they go? Home, to part-time jobs at places like McDonald's, the stores downtown or at the Mall.

The Mall. Right.

Sooner or later, everybody went to the Mall. To work in the stores or to hang out.

The Avenger sighed, dreading the prospect of going to the Mall every day but knowing that he had no other choice.

For the next three weeks, he went to the Mall almost every afternoon that his chores permitted him to go. He stationed himself for periods of time at the entrance, then walked through the place, looking, always looking, but acting as if he was not looking, trying not to act suspicious. But how do you do that? He figured that it was best to look natural, not to lurk behind the fake birches or the huge ferns placed here and there in the Mall. He did not stay in one spot too long, either, and whistled softly, looking at his watch occasionally, as if he were waiting for someone. Meanwhile, his eyes were like secret cameras, taking pictures of the guys going by or standing around in groups, his eyes darting here, there, and everywhere.

He learned to avoid the security guards, although they were not a problem. Even though they wore impressive uniforms, they were old, weary-looking, retired police officers, maybe. But The Avenger still avoided them, moving on if one of them approached. Meanwhile, he kept looking, searching, ignoring his aching head, his sore eyes.

Once in a while, his heart leaped in his chest as he spotted a face that looked familiar. This happened a few times. He would follow the guy, squinting, trying to get a clear look at him, trying to superimpose the face of a trasher on the suspicious face. He was always disappointed: it was never a trasher. Then a terrible thought: Suppose he had already seen one of the trashers but had not recognized him? Suppose his memory was faulty? Impossible, he told himself. He was The Avenger. Whenever he closed his eyes, even in the turmoil of the Mall, he could bring forth the faces of the trashers, the way they had walked and talked and yelled, the way they had looked, without any doubt at all.

But where were they?

He went into the stores, looking at the clerks, and learned that most of the clerks were girls, especially in the department stores. He spotted boys carrying boxes or pushing carts piled high with merchandise. Guys worked in the food places—McDonald's, Papa Gino's, Friendly's. The Avenger got sick of eating pizzas and hamburgers, although he would not have thought that possible before his vigils at the Mall.

One day he saw Jane Jerome. His heart swelled up, seemed too big for his chest. Then began to pound. She was beautiful. She did not see him. He could not take his eyes from her. Like those nights when he used to watch her in her bedroom. She'd pull down the window shade but not all the way, leaving an inch or so at the bottom. The Avenger watched her through that inch. Saw her doing her homework, the pencil tip between her lips. Full lips, pink. Saw her undressing. Taking off her blouse, revealing her white lacy bra. Dropping her skirt to the floor. She never picked up her clothes, left them draped over a chair, or flung on the bed, or simply to the floor, a puddle of skirt, blouses, or sweaters. She sometimes walked around in her bra and panties. He felt his eyes bulging. Felt hot and cold at the same time. Like chills and fever. Could hear his breath going in and out. He wondered if she knew he was watching at the window. Was performing for him, walking around almost naked. He blinked, confused. What if she took off her bra and panties? He had never seen a naked woman before. Did not know what he would do if she took off everything. But it was impossible for Jane Jerome to do something like that. Not his Jane. She was not like other girls. Not like her sister who did not even say hello to him

when she walked by, always in a hurry, never stopped t
speak to him. He would not bother looking into *her* win
dow. But at Jane's window, he always felt strange—shiver
ing and warm at the same time, hoping she would take of
her bra and panties and yet not wanting her to do tha
Only a bad girl would parade herself around knowing tha
someone was watching at the window. And Jane was no
bad. As she tugged at the top of her panties, pulling ther
tight around her behind, he wondered: was she bad, afte
all?

One night, he found the shade pulled all the wa
down. Still down the next night. And all the other night
afterward. He was sad at first, as if he had lost somethin
precious, and then he was relieved. You must resist temp
tation, his mother always said. He knew that Jane must b
temptation, especially with the shade up.

Seeing her now in the Mall, he faded into the shadow
under the escalator, watching her pass, eating her up wit
his eyes. Everything bright and shining about her. The wa
her body moved when she walked. Her hair bouncing. Sh
had tied it at the back of her head in a ponytail and i
bounced gently as she walked. He liked the back of he
neck, the white skin peeking out of the wisps of hair. Wh
does she make me feel feverish? he wondered. She's only
girl. She entered a store, out of sight, and he was bot
relieved and sad.

The Avenger began to dream of the Mall at nigh
Dreamed of himself walking through the place like it was
museum all black and white and the kids standing aroun
like statues. Statues with big eyes staring at him. Followin
him as he walked by. He woke up sweating. And discour
aged. Which was unusual because The Avenger never al
lowed himself to be discouraged. But all those afternoon
at the Mall had been without success. Maybe the trasher

were not from around the Wickburg area. Maybe they
came from places like Boston or Providence. Too far away.
He groaned, tossing in the bed. How could he track them
down in Boston? Or, wait, maybe they were just lying low.
Keeping out of sight. Maybe they suspected that The
Avenger had seen them that night and were staying away
from public places. That could be the answer. Which
meant that he would have to be patient again. Watch and
wait. Bide his time. Wait for the means and the opportunity. It had worked before. With Vaughn Masterson and
his grandfather. It would work again. He was The Avenger
and The Avenger never failed.

He fell asleep and his dreams were sweet this time,
although he could not remember them when he woke up in
the morning.

"They've caught him," her father announced, coming
into the house, dropping his briefcase on the small table
next to the front door.

Jane and her mother were descending the stairs from
the second-floor bedrooms and said simultaneously:
"Caught who?" Like a comedy act on television.

But it wasn't comedy at all as they immediately realized who had been caught.

"One of the trashers," her father said. "The ring-
leader, in fact."

"Who is he?" Jane asked, strangely reluctant to hear
the answer. She was afraid that it might be someone she
knew, someone who was supposed to be a friend or a class-
mate at Burnside. Which would be worse than a stranger.

"Kid by the name of Harry Flowers. Lives in Wickburg. He's a senior at Wickburg Regional."

As her father talked Jane realized that something was
wrong. But what? The words were right. The way he spoke,

fast as usual, was also right. But something else was no
right at all.

"How did they catch him?" her mother asked.

"Jack Kelcey who lives around the corner on Vist
Drive? He just came back from a business trip to the Wes
Coast. He'd been gone almost a month and didn't know
about the trashing. When his wife told him about it, h
remembered seeing a car on the street that night. He'
been suspicious and actually wrote down the plate numbe:
Just in case. He's a methodical guy, keeps a small note
book, records everything. He didn't think any more abou
the car until he came home and heard about Karen an
the house. . . ."

Still something wrong, Jane thought.

"They traced the plate number to Wickburg. To a big
name architect. Winston Flowers, who's involved in design
ing condos. This kid is his son. . . ." Her father loosene
his tie. "The boy admits doing the damage. But he deni
touching Karen. Said she fell down the stairs. He also say
he was alone in the house, that nobody else was with him.

"But the police said there must have been at lea
three or four of them," her mother said, sinking to th
bottom step of the stairway.

Finally, Jane knew what was wrong.

"He claims he was alone although he's obviously l
ing," her father said. "He's probably also lying about n
touching Karen." Her father hesitated, still fumbling wi
his tie. "Thing is—the police don't have much to go on."

"Much to go on?" her mother said, rising to her fe
again, voice shrill with anger. "Karen in a coma, what h
did to this house, Mr. Kelcey who saw his car and he a
mits being here. What else do they need?"

Her father frowned, perspiration glistening on h

forehead, face flushed. He patted his pockets as if searching for cigarettes, although he had not smoked in years.

"The police have to go according to the evidence," her father explained. "There is no direct evidence that he touched Karen. The boy denies it and Karen can't testify. There is no evidence that he was *not* alone. There is no evidence that he broke into the house so they couldn't arrest him for breaking and entering . . ."

This is what was wrong: her father had not looked at her since he had entered the house. Had looked only at her mother, as if Jane weren't here, did not exist.

"Dad . . ." Jane began, chilly suddenly as if someone had left a window open and a cold wind was blowing across her flesh, causing goose pimples.

But her mother interrupted, still indignant, face flushed: "Why can't they arrest him for breaking into this place? He was in here, wasn't he? He admitted doing the damage, didn't he?"

"There were no signs of forced entry," her father said slowly, pacing the words, emphasizing each word separately, as if he were writing on a blackboard.

"What does *that* mean?" Jane's mother asked.

While a shadow crossed Jane's mind.

"It means," her father said, still not looking at Jane, "that he didn't have to break into this house. Didn't have to break a window or break down a door."

"Then how did he get in?"

Look at me, Jane wanted to shout, why won't you look at me? But stood there, silent, in dread, a stranger in her own home.

"Because he simply walked in," her father said, voice harsh and dry, as if his throat hurt. "He had a key to the house. He put the key in the lock, opened the door and walked in."

"A key to this house, *our* house? In heaven's name how would he get a key?"

For the first time since he arrived home, Jane's father looked at her. Looked directly into her eyes, his own eyes flashing with—what?—anger? More than anger. She groped for the word and, to her horror, found it. Accusation. That's what she saw in his eyes.

"He said that Jane gave him the key." His voice flat, the voice of a stranger.

Standing in the hallway of her home with her mother and father, while a lawn mower whirred away someplace in the neighborhood, Jane Jerome suddenly knew what the end of the world would be like.

PART TWO

Marty Sanders was waiting for Buddy when he stepped off the bus in front of Wickburg Regional the next morning. A dull ache in his head and his eyes stinging from the morning sun, Buddy grimaced as Marty's foghorn voice greeted him:

"Hung over?" Fake concern in his eyes.

Buddy did not bother to answer. He saw Randy Pierce lurking near the school's entrance, bland as usual, as if waiting for someone to draw an expression on his face.

Marty drew Buddy aside and spoke out of the corner of his mouth like a gangster in some cheap old movie. "Bad news, Buddy."

The other students streamed by them, one guy jostling Buddy with his elbow. The bus emitted stenches of exhaust.

Trying to figure the categories of bad news, he came up with a name: Harry Flowers. The dull ache in his head intensified into a sharp pain that embraced his entire skull. The sun made him blink. He looked toward Randy, whose face was a sunspot.

"Harry was picked up yesterday by the cops," Marty said. "Rang the bell at his house about four o'clock and hauled him off to the police station. Arrested him for vandalism—that house in Burnside we hit . . ."

Buddy moaned, a strange alien sound he barely recognized as his own as he watched the bus lumbering away. *We Are Sunk. The End.*

"Don't worry," Marty said, confidential, face so close to Buddy's that a pimple near his nose looked like a crater on the moon. "Harry won't tell. He's not a squealer."

Tell, squeal. Fifth-grade words.

"Everybody squeals," Buddy said, but what he meant was: *I would squeal. I wouldn't want to squeal but I'd do it. I would break down and admit everything.*

"Look, Buddy," Marty said, voice deeper than ever, if that was possible. "I've known Harry all my life. We were in preschool together. Harry never double-crosses his friends."

But I am not his friend. I could never be his friend.

"Have you talked to him?" Buddy asked.

"Just a quick talk. He called last night, about eight when he got home. He said not to worry, he was taking the blame. He won't be in school today—has to go back to the police station today. With his father. He said his father's going to make restitution for the damage, doesn't want to make waves, doesn't want publicity. Which lets us off the hook. Harry said he'd call me tonight with the details."

In the distance Randy nodded his head, as if he could hear what Marty was saying.

I could use a drink. Even at eight-ten in the morning. Even though a drink this early would make him sick to his stomach.

"How did the police find out about him?" Buddy asked, barely aware that the first warning bell had sounded, usually the loudest bell in the world that jolted most students into an instant run for the front door.

"Harry said a witness saw his car that night."

"What witness?" Buddy asked. "And why did he wait so long? It's been more than three weeks." Three weeks plus five days—Buddy knew exactly when the trashing had occurred.

"I don't know," Marty said, leading Buddy toward the school's entrance, where Randy greeted them, a sickly smile on his face now, the smile like a bandage covering a wound. "All I know is that Harry said not to worry. And he's a man of his word."

In the first place, he's not a man. He's a high school senior. And what do I know about his word? Buddy looked over his shoulder, as if expecting to see a police cruiser streak toward the school, turning on the siren the instant the cops spotted them.

"If the witness saw Harry, he probably saw us," Buddy said.

Randy finally spoke: "We don't know if the witness is a *he* or a *she.*"

"Stop splitting hairs, for ˚crissakes," Marty said to Randy. "Who cares if the witness is a he or a she?" The kind of stupid argument Marty and Randy usually carried on. "The witness, *he* or *she*"—emphasizing the words for Randy's benefit—"saw the car. Got the license plate number. The cops traced it to Harry's house." Still talking sarcastically to Randy, as if speaking to a little kid. "They didn't think his father had done the damage. Middle-aged guys don't ordinarily get their kicks trashing houses. So they arrested Harry." Snorting with contempt as he shook his head.

The second warning bell sounded, clanging inside Buddy's head. Two minutes remaining to get inside the place and to their lockers. Then to their homerooms for attendance.

"Relax, Buddy," Marty croaked, his voice more like a bullfrog's now than a foghorn. "Harry won't let us down."

Famous last words, Buddy thought as they pushed their way into the school. His locker contained a hidden half pint of gin that he kept for emergencies. He wondered whether he had enough time to sneak a couple of gulps. He felt in his jacket pocket for Life Savers. Despite his throbbing head and queasy stomach, he needed the easing of tension and dread the gin would supply while waiting for the cops to come and take him off to jail.

That evening, he leaped with alarm when a knock came at his bedroom door. The cops, he thought. His mother, grim-faced, greeted him as he reluctantly opened the door. "Could I have a word with you, Buddy?" She knows, he thought, as his face grew warm, like shame made visible. "Addy's in my bedroom, waiting . . ."

He followed her there and found Addy sitting on the dainty delicate chair in front of his mother's dressing table. Addy shot him a look of curiosity, as if saying: I don't know what this is all about, either.

Hands on hips, shoulders stiff, as if standing at attention, his mother drew a deep breath and said: "I'm thinking of going away for a few days. . . ."

Buddy sagged against the wall, a surge of relief flowing through him, as if he'd had a fever that had suddenly stopped. Then wondered in a panic: Is she leaving us, too? He looked at Addy but found no answer in her eyes.

As if reading his mind, his mother said: "No, I'm not moving out or anything like that. And I'm not taking a vacation, either. I'm thinking of going on a retreat. . . ."

The word echoed vaguely in Buddy's mind, something to do with religion and prayer. But he asked the question anyway: "What's a retreat?" And immediately felt stupid as usual when involved in a conversation with his mother and Addy.

"It's a place to go for meditation and prayer," Addy explained but not in a wise guy voice, trying to be helpful.

"Exactly," his mother said. "It's a five-day retreat, a long weekend, Friday through Tuesday at a kind of monastery south of Worcester." She sank down on the bed. "I've got to get myself together. I mean, I've only been going through the motions, at work, here at home with the two of you. During the retreat, I'll have a chance to think. To meditate, pray. There's a counselor. I'll be going with a group of women from all walks of life."

"That's just great, Mom," Addy said heartily.

And Buddy echoed the word: "Great." Trying to inject it with enthusiasm.

"We'll get along fine," Addy said. "We'll load up on frozen stuff, order Chinese goop, and I can make my specialties . . ."

"Meat loaf and shake-and-bake chicken," Buddy said, chiding her pleasantly, wanting to be a part of her cheerfulness and his mother's decision. At the same time, he looked searchingly at his mother, trying to see her not as his mother but as a woman. A troubled, unhappy woman. Saw the small network of lines at the corners of her eyes, the thin, downturned lips. Had her lips always been so thin? Had she always looked this way? Sadness made him take his eyes away from her. Since his father's departure, his mother had been only a presence in the house, as insubstantial as a shadow. He had awakened each day thinking, today somehow we'll talk, I'll ask her how she's doing, how she's *really* doing, we'll get past all that polite table talk and get things out in the open. But as each day wore on, and the booze took hold, his morning vow dissolved.

His mother remained preoccupied, distant at the table a
though she talked—how she talked—but mechanical tall
about work, inquiring about school, but not absorbing th
answers, distracted.

"Look, kids," she said now. "Maybe I haven't been th
best wife and mother and I've also been a lousy Catholic
Your father did his best for you. He went along with all th
demands of the Church when we married. Agreed that ou
children would be brought up Catholic, although I decide
at one point that you both should make your decision
about religion and what to be."

When did that happen? Buddy wondered. All he kne
was that at some point in his life, his mother had stoppe
going to mass and they had stopped too. And she did no
insist on those boring religion classes anymore. Was tha
one of Addy's sins of omission?

"I have to do something," she continued, sittin
straight on the bed, her hands stroking the spread. "And
have to start somewhere. The other day I realized it wa
either a psychiatrist or a retreat. Maybe it'll be both in th
end." She closed her eyes. "All I want is a little peace.'
Tears oozed past her closed eyelids.

"Oh, Mom," Addy cried, and flung herself at he
mother, kneeling on the floor, her arms around he
mother's waist. Buddy envied them, together like that. En
vied his mother, who might find that peace she wanted o
retreat. Envied Addy, who could embrace her mother pas
sionately, live passionately, writing plays, doing things
While he waited for the cops to show up, which woul
bring disgrace to them all.

But the cops never came.

Three days later, just before supper, Harry called, tell
ing Buddy—not asking but *telling* him—that he would pic
him up at eight o'clock.

"Time to have a talk," Harry said, voice dry and crisp with no sign of an accent.

Buddy's hand stayed on the phone for a long time after he hung up.

The Avenger was angry, almost in tears—not childish tears but tears of anger and frustration—as he sat on the bus on the way home from the Mall. He knew that he would not go to the Mall anymore in his search for the trashers. He was tired of looking, looking, but never seeing them. A few minutes ago, a security guard had approached him as he stood across from the escalators trying not to act suspicious, acting as if he were waiting for his mother to show up. The guard was old with red blemishes like small flowers on his cheeks, but his eyes were dark and watchful. He did not speak to The Avenger but stood close to him. Too close. When The Avenger moved on, the guard moved with him. The Avenger did not know whether this was a coincidence or whether the guard did not want him hanging around the Mall. The Avenger finally slipped through the revolving doors with the knowledge that he would not return to the Mall anymore. Three weeks of looking had failed to turn up any of the trashers.

As the bus lumbered down Main Street, The Avenger pondered his next move. Maybe he should start visiting the high schools, although he knew that this was almost impossible to undertake. A lot of schools in the area. Too many. Why hadn't the trashers shown up at the Mall the way hundreds of other guys did? He beat his fist against the window until his knuckles hurt and an old woman in the seat in front of him turned and frowned at him. She wore thick glasses that magnified her eyes. He looked bleakly out of the window at the stores passing by. Felt helpless, unable to proceed with his plans for revenge. Anger stirred inside him, his heel drummed the floor, and the old woman shuffled her shoulders and half glanced back at him again. He realized he had been hitting the back of her seat with his knee.

Making an effort to keep his knee from moving, his foot from tapping the floor, his knuckles from hitting the window, he put on his thinking cap. The cap was tight on his head, like a real cap, too small for his skull. He closed his eyes, carried along by the bumping and thumping of the bus. He dreaded to wonder what Jane would think if she knew he had failed her, had failed to find the trashers.

Sadness replaced his anger. Sadness, because he could not spy on the Jeromes anymore even though he did not consider himself a spy. He had been an observer. By observing them, he had become part of the family. But with the shrubbery all gone now and the branches of the old oak trees trimmed back, the house looked naked, exposed to the world. No more hiding places for him to look at the family.

In his months of observation, he had come to love them. That's why he had done the things he had done. Because of that love. *You always hurt the one you love.* That was a song his mother always sang. An old song. Her theme song, sort of. When she lost her patience and punished him, those words echoed in his mind. This is for your own good, she would say. And he would think: You always hurt the one you love. So when he began to love the Jeromes, he knew that he had to hurt them, to show them his love. Even though it made him feel bad to do things. Things like yanking Mrs. Jerome's tomato plants out of the garden, which hurt not only her but *him* as well, because he loved to see the brave and pretty plants sunning themselves. Plus putting the dead squirrel in the mailbox. The Avenger had not killed the squirrel—he had found it by the side of the road, hit by a car, no doubt. He would never kill a helpless animal, especially a small one.

Now the anger was gone and so was the sorrow as the bus left downtown Wickburg and made its way to the outskirts where Burnside awaited him. He had nothing but a vast emptiness inside of him. Like hunger, although it had nothing to do with eating food. Hunger for—what? Action. To do something. The old woman had gotten off the bus— he had not noticed her departure—and now a young lady sat in the seat in front of him. She had a small baby in her arms. The baby began to fuss a bit and the young lady hoisted the baby up to her shoulder and the baby looked at him. The baby started to cry, face all scrunched up in its bonnet. Was the baby a boy or a girl? He couldn't tell. But he wished the baby would stop crying and stop staring at him.

He looked away, out the window, at the houses with their lawns and cars parked in driveways and the baby stopped crying. But when he looked again, the baby was looking at him. Did babies have some kind of special power when they looked at people? Ridiculous, of course. But who could tell what babies were thinking? This baby had dark eyes like the security guard at the Mall. The baby looked at him with those dark eyes, face all wrinkled like a paper bag that had been crushed in somebody's hand. He did not like the way the baby was staring at him and looked out the window again. He also began to get angry again. Angry at the Mall which he had always hated and hated even more now because the trashers had not gone there. Angry, too, at this baby staring at him. And the baby's mother paying no attention at all. He wondered if the mother would pay attention if he did something to the baby.

The bus lurched again, hitting a bump in the road and came to a stop. The doors hissed open and closed and the young lady got up. She did not get off the bus but took another seat in the front of the bus near the door. The Avenger told himself to take it easy, not to get angry again. But why did she change her seat? Did the baby's mother have powers of her own? Did she read The Avenger's mind as he sat behind her? He looked out the window again, hitting the glass with his knuckles, not caring whether he was making noise or not. He told himself to get rid of these thoughts. How could that lady read his mind anyway? And what special powers could a little baby have? Ridiculous. And yet . . .

He was relieved when the bus arrived at downtown Burnside. He got off the bus without looking at the young lady and the baby. He should focus on the trashers and not strangers. He shivered as he considered what he might have done to that baby. He was in a hurry now to get to the shed and map out new plans. What kind of new plans? He wasn't sure. He glanced in the window of a hardware store and looked at the tools. Hammers and saws—like weapons waiting for his use. Maybe he should start a collection while waiting for the trashers. Round up all the weapons he could find. Excitement rose in him and he almost bumped into a man who was standing in front of a drug-store reading a newspaper. The newspaper fluttered in the air like a soiled flag.

"Excuse me," The Avenger said in his polite way, excitement making his blood race now. Knives and guns and axes and pliers in his thoughts.

Because The Avenger seldom read a newspaper he would never know that the newspaper the man had been holding carried a story with the headline

ARCHITECT'S SON

ADMITS VANDALISM

* * *

"Harry's glad you're here," Harry Flowers said as they sat in his car two streets away from Buddy's house. Buddy preferred this spot rather than some public place. He did not want to be seen by anyone, particularly the police, in the company of Harry Flowers.

"Harry thought you might have better things to do." That same phony voice. Buddy hated people, like ball players and politicians, who referred to themselves in the third person. He shrugged, did not feel particularly like talking. Let Harry Flowers carry the ball. This meeting was his idea, anyway.

Silence gathered in the car as dusk deepened into the first stages of night, the streetlights brightening in the gathering darkness.

"Have a drink," Harry said, offering a half pint of gin he had pulled out of the glove compartment.

Buddy wanted to refuse, wished desperately that he could refuse, but he needed all the defenses possible when talking to Harry Flowers and he accepted the bottle, took a tentative gulp, then a good healthy swallow, grimacing as usual at the taste, the burning in his throat.

He handed the bottle back to Harry and noticed dimly that Harry did not take a drink.

"Tell me something, Buddy, why don't you trust Harry?"

The question surprised Buddy. But Harry always was capable of the surprise, the verbal ambush.

"What makes you think I don't trust you?" Buddy asked, hoping the gin would do its work quickly, relaxing

him so that he would be able to hold his own with Harry
Flowers in what promised to be a delicate conversation.

Harry handed him the bottle again. Buddy hesitated,
still wanting to refuse it but giving in. Christ, he always
gave in. As he raised the bottle to his lips, he stalled before
drinking, studying Harry's face.

Buddy could not deny the fact that Harry had kept his
word, had shouldered the blame for the trashing without
naming anyone else. His father had paid for the damages.
Sat down and wrote a big check without quibbling, according to Marty. Throughout the week, Buddy had waited for
the phone to ring, a knock on the door, a summons to
police headquarters. None of that had happened. A three-
paragraph story on the inside page of the newspaper ran
under a modest headline in small type:

ARCHITECT'S SON
ADMITS VANDALISM

The brief story gave no details, only the names of
Harry and his father, and reported that restitution had
been made, Harry placed on probation. Did not mention
the name of the family whose home was vandalized and
omitted any reference to the girl who had been pushed
down the stairs.

"Admit it, Buddy. You thought Harry would blow the
whistle on you and Marty and Randy," Harry said.

Swallowing the booze, eyes watering a bit, Buddy knew
he could not deny the truth of Harry's statement.

"Of course, I don't blame you for that," Harry continued. He had dropped the third-person Harry: "The kind of
world we're living in nobody expects you to do the right
thing. . . ."

"Okay, Harry," Buddy heard himself saying. "I appre-

ciate what you did. I really do. I think it's great . . ."
Buddy groped for more words and could not find them.

"Big statement," Harry said. "But you ran out of
steam there, Buddy. Know why? Because you were about
to add *but*. *Hell, I think it's a great thing you did, Harry, but
. . .* What the *but* means, Buddy, is you're looking for the
angle. You're figuring that I must have an ulterior motive
for what I did. Right?"

"But *why* did you do it, Harry?" Buddy asked, giving in
to his curiosity. "Why did you take all the blame? How did
you get your father to pay the entire bill? We did as much
damage as you did. Maybe more." The booze was beginning to work and he thought of the girl's room, the exhilaration of ripping her posters from the wall, sweeping her
knickknacks from the shelf, tearing her bed apart.

"Is it so hard to understand?" Harry asked. "Am I
supposed to be a bad guy or something? Sure, I like to
raise a little hell, have a good time, smoke a little pot,
drink a little booze. Does that make me a prize heel? Hey,
Buddy, I'm good to my mother and don't hassle my father.
I make the honor roll. My folks appreciate all that. And
when I got into trouble, my father helped out. My father
loves me. He wrote the check and asked no questions."

Buddy glanced again at Harry. Harry Flowers, good
student, good son, good guy. *What's wrong with this picture?
Or was there anything wrong?*

"I'm sorry," he said, the booze making it easy to say
the words again.

"You don't have to be sorry. Just accept what I did for
what it was. I wasn't trying to be a hero. I just did what I
thought was best for all of us. Why drag my friends into a
mess when it wasn't necessary?"

But I'm not your friend. Didn't that make Harry's ges-
ture even more noble then? Buddy had always thought in

terms of good and evil, that you were either good or bad
And he automatically placed himself in the category of
good guys. Which made Harry a bad guy, automatically
Now he wasn't certain, not certain about anything about
himself. A good guy didn't do rotten things. And he, Buddy
Walker, good guy, had helped wreck a family's house. He
also drank in secret, went to school drunk sometimes
Missed the honor roll. Harry made the honor roll. Buddy's
father had left home, abandoned his family while Harry's
father loved him, *My father loves me,* and was willing to pay
the damages for Harry's vandalism.

"What's the matter?" Harry asked.

"Nothing," Buddy answered. But, yes, there was some
thing.

"I know what's bothering you," Harry said.

Buddy turned to him, alarmed. Could Harry read his
thoughts? Harry had always been capable of surprises—
was this another one?

"You're wondering how I got away with it, right? Why
the judge gave me probation, why there was so little public
ity, why the charge against me was so minor? Is that what's
bothering you?"

The gin spoke for Buddy: "Right, yes, that's exactly
what I was wondering." But thinking: no, I wasn't wonder
ing about that at all, relieved that Harry, after all, was no
a mind reader.

"You see, Buddy, they *had* to believe me and go along
with what I said." Harry's customary coolness had vanished
and he actually seemed excited as he talked. "They had no
choice."

"Why did they have no choice?" Buddy asked, sensing
that he was playing into Harry's hands like a straight man
in a comedy act.

"Well, actually, they *thought* they had a choice

'hought they could throw the book at me. Breaking and
ntering. Malicious damage to property. Assaulting the
irl. But as it turned out, they had to forget most of the
harges. No breaking and entering, no assaulting the girl.
'hat left them only with damage to property. Also, I'm
nly eighteen, from a respectable family, no previous ar-
ests."

"But the girl is in the hospital, Harry. In a coma. How
ould they overlook that?"

"They didn't overlook it. They just didn't blame me. I
old them that she fell down the stairs. Came rushing in the
ouse in the dark and opened the wrong door. When she
omes out of the coma—*if* she comes out of the coma"—
distinction that gave Buddy the shivers—"it's her
ord against mine. Besides, there were mitigating circum-
ances. Know what mitigating circumstances are, Buddy?"
Iarry handed him the bottle again.

Buddy sipped, floating with the booze now, but some-
ow his mind sharp and clear. "Tell me, Harry." Fasci-
ated, despite the revulsion he felt.

"Mitigating circumstances means that I came up with
ie clincher. And the clincher made all the difference in
ie world. You must always have a clincher, Buddy, and I
ad the clincher even before we went into that house."

Buddy knew that Harry was waiting for the next ques-
on and Buddy supplied it, speaking slowly and carefully:
What was the clincher, Harry?"

"The key, Buddy," Harry proclaimed, triumph in his
oice. "I had a key to the house. The key opened the front
oor. As a result, no charge of breaking and entering. Re-
iember the order I gave: Don't break any windows. That's
hy, Buddy. So that they couldn't say we broke into the
lace. . . ."

Buddy flashed back to that night, remembering how

Harry had parked the car on a quiet neighborhood stree
whispered "Wait here" and disappeared around the co
ner. Reappearing a few minutes later, he beckoned Budd
Marty, and Randy from the corner, maybe a hundred fe
away. Befuddled by the booze, Buddy had been only mild
curious about the ease with which Harry ushered them
the Jerome house, the front door open, lights on inside. H
had quickly forgotten his curiosity as the vandalism bega

"That's why it went so easy in court, Buddy. That
why, when my father agreed to restitution, everybody we
along, the judge and the cops. I pleaded nolo contender
Know what nolo means? It means I admitted to the facts
the case without admitting guilt. Neat, right? A bit of leg
sleight of hand, my father's lawyer said. The judge place
me on probation and my father paid up. . . ."

Something was wrong here, something was missin
"How about the other family, Harry? Why did they g
along? Didn't they want to see justice done? Their hou
wrecked? Their daughter in the hospital?"

"Her father was there all the time, Buddy. And he wa
ready to blow his top. Or bust a gut. I thought at one poi
that he was going to jump over the guardrail and atta
me. But he didn't. He couldn't. He had no choice. . . ."

"Because you had a key to the house," Buddy said, sti
a bit puzzled. Suddenly, he knew what had been missin
"How did you get the key, Harry?"

Harry smiled expansively, leaning back. "I told the
the girl gave it to me. The man's daughter." A chortle
triumph in his voice.

Buddy recoiled as if Harry had struck him. "That gi
the one who . . ."

"Not the girl in the hospital," Harry said. "Two gir
live in that house. The other one. Her name is Jane. Jan
Jerome . . ."

"She gave you the key to her house?" Buddy asked, unable to keep the disbelief from his voice.

"You're not paying attention, Buddy. I said I told them he gave me the key. Notice the difference?"

Buddy nodded, sober suddenly, all wooziness gone, the pleasant drifting over, and a headache asserting itself, throbbing dully above his eyes.

"How did you get the key?"

"Simple," he said. "Picture this: I'm in the Mall one afternoon and I see a girl pull her wallet out of her pocket. A key falls to the floor. She doesn't see it fall. Because I'm such a gentleman"—and he leered at Buddy with such an evil grin that Buddy flinched—"I went over and picked up the key. Was going to give it to her. But she was walking away, into the Pizza Palace. I watched her go, holding the key in my hand. Looked at it. What kind of key was this? Didn't look like a car key. What other key would a girl her age have? Locker key at school? Most lockers have combinations. No. Must be—*voilà*—her house key, the key to her home." Harry paused and his voice grew dreamy. "Funny thing happened, Buddy. I thought: Here I hold the key to her house in my hand. This key can open the door to her house, to her family, to her private life. Christ, what a feeling. So I followed her into the Pizza Palace, made a few inquiries about her. And found out that her name was Jane Jerome and she lived in Burnside. . . ." He waved his hand in the air. "The rest is history. . . ."

Then, turning to him, serious again: "Listen, how I got the key is not important. What's important is the *effect* the key had on everybody at the police station. One minute everybody is ready to make all kinds of charges. Next minute, they say: Whoa, let's take another look at this case. Her father pulls the cops aside. His face is the color of ashes in a barbecue pit. I know what her father is saying, know what he's thinking. He's thinking headlines. Like GIRL AIDS IN VANDALISM OF HER OWN HOME. Her picture in the paper, on television maybe. See, Buddy? See why they had to believe me, why her father agreed to the lesser charges, accepted the restitution without making waves? Why the cops decided to believe I was alone? Everybody was suddenly glad to have it all over with. . . ."

It wasn't until later, long after Harry had driven off and Buddy was crawling into bed, hoping the Pepto-Bismol would ease his nausea, that he thought:

But how about the girl?

Hey, Harry, how about the girl?

Seven hours and twenty minutes (she did not keep track of the seconds). The longest seven hours of her life. She spent them all in her room. Did not open the door when her mother knocked and called her name. Did not respond when her father rattled the doorknob and pleaded with her to come out.

"Please, Jane," he said, his voice strangled. "Please come out. Let's talk about this."

She did not answer, merely sat on her legs, knees crossed in front of her—like a wistful Buddha. "Hey, Jane," Artie called once, after rapping his knuckles on the door, their secret signal to each other: three short raps, two long, when they used to try to outwit baby-sitters in the olden days when they were young. "Don't be a sap, Jane. Come on out."

She did not answer Artie, either. *Don't be a sap, Jane.* Where did he get that word, *sap,* anyway? Stupid word.

She did not like her room anymore. Missed her posters. Most of her small glass animals had been spared damage but she refused to put them on display again. They were tucked away in tissue paper in a box on the closet shelf. She always carefully stepped over that spot near the door where the vomit had lain in a terrible puddle.

She sniffed, wrinkling her nose, seeking that foul odor under the surface of things. No odor now but she knew it lurked there, threatening to emerge when she least expected it.

"The key," she muttered. "The damn key."

She went to the window, looked out, surprised to find that rain was falling. She'd heard no raindrops on the windowpane. Soft, gentle spring rain, a melancholy rain, the street deserted, no children playing, no dogs in sight. Were trashers lingering in the woods?

She should have told her parents about the key immediately. As soon as she realized she had lost it. But she'd been losing things around that time. Her red leather wallet, a Christmas gift, that she'd somehow lost with twenty dollars in Christmas money inside. Lost it at the movies. Two days later, the theater called, reporting that the wallet had been found. It was damaged, torn, and money gone, of course. Next, she had lost a pearl earring, another gift from her favorite aunt, Aunt Cassie, back in Monument. Didn't mention it to anyone. Her mother had found it in a corner of the kitchen floor. Which made it worse. "Didn't you know it was missing?" her mother had asked. "Why didn't you tell us?" Then to Jane's father: "Know what's happening, Jerry? Our kids are keeping secrets from us."

All of which surprised Jane. Didn't her parents know that all kids kept secrets from their parents? Hadn't her mother and father done the same thing when they were kids? Or did growing up cause a kind of amnesia about stuff like that?

When she lost the key, she kept quiet about it. Did not mention it to anyone even though Karen and Artie probably would have helped her look for it. Actually, there did not seem to be any serious need for a key. Most of the time, somebody was home when Jane arrived. The key was a pain in the neck. She had no other keys. No car key—she was taking Driver's Ed. at school, did not drive her father's car yet. Combination lock on her school locker; she kept her house key either in her pocket or in one of the slots of her wallet. Half the time she couldn't find it. Sometimes it slipped out of her jeans pocket into the chair. When she discovered it was missing, she wasn't sure when or where she had lost it. That was another reason for her delay in reporting the loss; she couldn't have supplied any details. In time, she completely forgot about the key. Even when the trashing occurred, she did not connect it with her missing key.

"Jane."

Her mother.

What Jane could not forget: the way her father had refused to look at her, had kept ignoring her, as if she had been barred from the family. When finally he *did* look at her, his eyes were the eyes of a stranger. An accusing stranger. Until that moment, she had not realized how the eyes contain the secret of who you are and what you are. Looking into her father's eyes, she had seen a stranger, the man other people met on the street or at the office because the man in the front hallway was certainly not, for that blazing moment, repeat, *not* her father. *Her* father could never look at her that way, as if he, too, were seeing a stranger and not his daughter. A moment later, when he had uttered those terrible words, had asked that terrible question—*Did you give him the key?*—her mother had regarded her in the same way, her eyes like her father's but with surprise and befuddlement mixed in with the accusation.

Or was she being fair?

She had turned away, so quickly, so eager to get away from those accusing eyes, scurrying up the stairs, a sob escaping her lips, that she thought maybe she hadn't waited long enough for her father to offer an explanation for his behavior.

She looked at the clock. She had been in her room now for seven hours and thirty-two minutes. Had had no dinner—had not turned on her television set. Had not opened a book or played a disk on the CD. She had lived these past few hours like a hermit or a monk, fasting, keeping silent. In the first two or three hours, there had been no sounds from downstairs, not even a door closing or the muffled voices on television. The telephone did not even ring. Then, first her mother knocking and then her father. Taking turns.

Now her mother again:

"Know what you're doing, Jane?"

She did not answer but her silence asked: What *am* I doing?

"You're punishing us. For something you did."

They were still accusing her.

"Jane."

Her father's turn, his voice:

"You didn't give us enough time. I didn't say I *believed* that boy. I was only asking you, to hear you say it in your own words."

He hadn't asked. He had told her what the boy had said—that she gave him the key. She would never forget those words or his eyes or the way his voice had sounded.

"We know you didn't give him the key. We know you wouldn't do a thing like that."

And her mother: "You lost the key, didn't you? And you were afraid to tell us because you're always losing things. Right?"

She knew, of course, that her mother and father had been discussing the situation all this time, downstairs, in the kitchen, the living room, the way she had been agonizing here in her bedroom.

What she hated most of all was:

The trashing. The thing that had led her to this situation. Her friends Patti and Leslie gone, now her father a stranger and her mother his conspirator against her. How she hated them, those faceless trashers and that fellow Harry Something-or-other, who had lied and tried to implicate her in the trashing.

They were the enemy, not her father or mother. They were the reason she was a prisoner here in her own room. The reason her mother and father were in such agony.

She went to the door, turned the key, opened it. Saw her mother and father, their faces filled with apprehension and concern as they peered tentatively at her. In a moment, they were embracing, arms tangled around each other, cheeks damp, her mother whispering softly *Jane, Jane,* like a prayer, as if she had returned from a long trip, her father pressing her close to him, as if he had to feel the contours of her body to be sure she was there.

She gave in to their ministrations, letting herself go, basking in the circle of their love and their warmth and their comfort, but in a small distant part of herself, wondering if things would ever be the same again.

"I'm sorry."

A whisper of a voice, soft, distant, as if coming from a faraway country, another planet.

"Who is this?" she asked, puzzled, wary, wondering if she had misunderstood what the voice had said. *I'm sorry.* For what? "What did you say?"

She was alone in the house. After school. When the

phone rang she'd picked it up automatically, without any thought about who might be calling. Nobody called her these days. That's why the ringing of the phone didn't excite her as it did when she had that stupid crush on Timmy Kearns and the days when Patti and Leslie had been her friends.

"Is this Jane Jerome?" the voice asked. A boy's voice, kind of breathless as if he had been running a long distance.

"Yes," she said. "Who is this?" A slight quiver of fear now in her voice. *I should hang up.* Ever since the vandalism, fear had crouched under the surface of everyday events, whether it was the ringing of the doorbell or an unfamiliar face on the street or someone who seemed to be staring at her at the supermarket checkout line. Now this unknown voice on the phone.

She was about to hang up when a soft sigh came over the line, the kind of sigh a child makes at the end of a long weary day. And after the sigh, the same voice, tender now, saying: "I'm sorry about what happened."

Big pause.

Caught by surprise, she looked at the phone as if the instrument could provide the answer to who was calling. Then pressed it against her ear in time to hear the line go dead, followed by the blurting of the dial tone.

Her hand trembled as she replaced the receiver on its cradle. She stood there a moment, indecisive, trying to straighten out her thoughts. Her thoughts were all jumbled these days, as if her brain had short-circuited. Silly thought, of course, but she did not know how to express what had happened to her, what *was* happening to her.

She went to the window, blinked at the streams of sunshine against her eyeballs. Rain should be falling to suit her mood. Her black mood. She turned back from the window, hugged her arms around her chest, staring bleakly at each piece of furniture in the room. She found it hard these days to stay in the house at all. For a while, she found it difficult to be *alone* in the house and had fled the place. Now, she found it was almost impossible for her to be in the house even when her family was around. When her father glanced her way, she shriveled a bit. When he touched her shoulder and gave her a good-night peck on the cheek, she could not respond even though she knew this was wrong. But what he had done, doubting her, was also wrong. I've got to get over this, she told herself. But found it hard to do. She kept telling herself that her father was not the villain. The guy whose name was Harry Flowers had lied, had made her father doubt her.

Harry Flowers. She wondered about him. What did he look like? Was he tall or short? Fat or thin? What kind of person was he? What kind of person would do such terrible, sick things? She tried to picture him in her mind but he was a terrifying blank. Terrifying because she might have already met him, on the street, at a dance at school at the Mall, and did not know it. When she strolled the Mall, she looked curiously at the various fellows she met wondering: Is this him? She decided at one point to stay away from the Mall and then said: no. She would not let Harry Flowers control her life. He had already damaged her—her house, her feelings for her mother and father her life.

And now that phone call. That soft and gentle voice full of sorrow and regret. Someone out there who felt bad for her, who had tried to communicate how he felt. But why was he so mysterious? Why didn't he identify himself tell her his name? Was he—impossible—Harry Flowers? Calling to say he was sorry?

Harry Flowers seemed to have invaded her life, her

thoughts. The caller couldn't be him. He could not have faked such an apology. Not the Harry Flowers who had wreaked such havoc. Harry Flowers, Harry Flowers, Harry Flowers, she thought as she headed upstairs for a jacket and then to be out of here, out of this house. To where? Anywhere except here. Harry Flowers, Harry Flowers, Harry Flowers, the name filling her mind. Harry Flowers, Harry Flowers, Harry Flowers. Opening drawers, the closet, unbuttoning, buttoning. Harry Flowers, Harry Flowers, Harry Flowers. Combing her hair, hand shaking, shoulders shaking, body shaking. HarryFlowersHarryFlowersHarryFlowers. Maybe if she said his name long enough, fast enough, it would not be a name anymore, would lose all meaning, all power to threaten her. Harry Flowers Harryflowersharryflowersharryflowersharryflowersharryflowers . . . as she bounded down the steps and out the door into the outside world with harryflowersharryflowersharryflowersharryflowers . . . stop it stop it but could not could not harryflowersharryflowersharryflowersharryflowers until his name passed out of existence and became only syllables, a dim sound in her mind, then, thank God, nothing.

The instant he heard her voice he remembered her face. Everything happened at once—the sound of her voice on the phone, then the flash of her features and the instant knowledge of where he had seen that face: in the picture on the bureau in that bedroom he had destroyed almost a month ago. He had completely forgotten about the picture in its chrome frame. He had been about to dash it against the wall when he paused, looked at the portrait of the girl for a long moment—dark hair falling to her shoulders, eyes slightly slanted, the hint of a smile on her lips but not quite a smile, as if she were trying to decide whether to smile or

not and the camera caught that hesitation. For some reason, he replaced the picture undamaged on the bureau
before continuing his frenzied assault on the room.

He had not given the picture another thought until:
Hello. And then: *Who is this?*

He had winced at the hesitancy in her voice, more than
that, her apprehension or maybe even fear, as if she was
afraid of whoever was on the other end of the line. Did she
answer all phone calls that way? *Is this what we did to her?*

Ever since Harry told him about the key, Buddy
couldn't stop thinking about the girl. Even though she had
been a cipher, a zero, blank, like a connect-the-dots face in
a comic-page puzzle. Then, he began to wonder about her.
How she must have felt walking into her bedroom and
seeing all that damage. *But I didn't pee against the wall,
somebody else did that.* He was surprised to find that he had
a girl on his mind whom he had never met. He had known
a lot of girls, but had never *had* a girl. Agonized over
crushes—although he was convinced they were not crushes
at the time but anguished love that would never end—
Alice Currier in the sixth grade with her hair like melting
caramel and Cindy Dennedy with whom he had his first
dance in the ninth grade and Debbie Howington, the love
of his life sophomore year, Debbie of the full tight sweaters and pouting lips who smiled at him one day and ignored him the next, who deigned to accept his invitation to
the movies one night and then called the next day to can-
cel, all of which caused him to shun the female sex, made
him think of becoming a monk in a monastery somewhere.
And here he was, all involved—in his thoughts, anyway—
with a girl he did not know, a girl he had never met but a
girl he knew collected small glass animals, had had a poster
of Billy Joel on her wall (which he had torn to shreds), a

girl Harry Flowers had used as a victim to protect himself as well as Marty and Randy. And Buddy, too.

That's why he found himself at the telephone that afternoon, woozy with the booze, filled with compassion for that poor poor girl, dialing the phone as if he were performing some tragic ritual, then astonished and shocked when he heard her voice.

As usual, when it came to the opposite sex, he had failed abysmally in what he had set out to do. Yet, he hadn't been quite sure what he had set out to do. Apologize? Not sure. But what else? He did not know.

After hanging up dismally, a failure at whatever he had planned to do, blaming the booze—he should have called when he was cold sober, icy (but then he wouldn't have had the nerve, would he?) and weary now with his thinking and drinking and his usual ineptitude, there was only one thing left to do:

Have another drink.

Which he did, of course, although it failed to erase the girl's face from the terrible thing his memory had become.

He began to follow her. Breaking his own rule and disregarding Addy's questioning glances, he drove his mother's car to school. Then, grateful that Wickburg Regional dismissed classes thirty minutes earlier than Burnside High, he drove to Burnside and waited for Jane Jerome to emerge. He followed slowly, almost stalling the car, as she walked to nearby Burnside Hospital where, he surmised, she visited her sister. He sat rigidly behind the wheel waiting for her to reappear, trying not to think of Karen Jerome in her hospital bed. Once or twice, he had telephoned the hospital to inquire about her condition. The answer invariably was an impersonal "Stable—no change."

Jane Jerome remained in the hospital for different periods of time—sometimes a few minutes, sometimes an hour or so, sometimes the remainder of the afternoon. On those days when she left the hospital after only a brief visit, she waited for the Wickburg Mall bus. Buddy then drove ahead, parked in the garage adjacent to the Mall, and was waiting for the bus when it disgorged passengers, Jane among them, at the Mall's entrance.

Following her from store to store, he tried to act casual, bought magazines which he pretended to read when she walked by only a few feet from him. She browsed leisurely, not buying anything, lingering at certain counters, pausing to riffle dresses hanging from the racks. He learned to be careful, to keep a certain distance, discovering in Filene's the danger of multiple mirrors. He came upon his reflection unexpectedly, startled to see himself reproduced in a dozen different angles, and almost panicked, wondering whether she had spotted him in one of the mirrors and was leading him on a merry chase.

Fleeing the store, he sat on a plastic yellow bench near the dry fountain, chipped and peeling, as if it were diseased. When she emerged from Filene's a few minutes later, she wandered toward the escalator. He watched her ascend to the second level, saw her moving along the second-floor guardrail, her head barely visible. After a minute or two, he stepped on the escalator and as he alighted, spotted her going into a bookstore at the far end of the corridor.

In the bookstore, he discovered the merits of peripheral vision: how you could see things without looking directly at them. He was able to open a book at the *Best Seller—20% Off* display and still see her in profile as she leafed through magazines ten feet away. When she closed a magazine with finality, he guessed that she was about to leave the store and he closed the book—he had no idea of its title or what it was about—and left the store before she did. That should convince her, if she had become suspicious, that he was not following her.

In front of the New Age Clothing store, he knelt on one knee as if checking the shoestrings of his Nikes and saw the flash of her legs as she passed by. He remained on his knee as she went beyond the escalator and continued to Marsh's, disappearing into the doorway. He waited awhile, counting to five hundred slowly, and then made his way into the store, walked warily through Housewares and Home Furnishings. She wasn't in sight. He checked out Women's Clothing and Summer Fun and even drifted through Men's Clothing before going to the down escalator. Halfway down, he spotted her below at the perfume counter, sampling the spray from a blue bottle. As he stepped off the escalator, she had drifted to the counter containing scarves and draped a red scarf across her chest before letting it settle back on the counter like a small collapsing tent.

Inhaling the remnants of perfume as he went by the counter, he looked for her without trying to look as if he were looking for her. Sighed impatiently at the sudden absurdity of what he was doing. Spying, for crissakes, on a girl he didn't know. Didn't see her anywhere—was she hiding behind a display case watching his befuddlement? He felt stupid, realizing the futility of what he had been doing. His legs were restless as he stood there, indecisive, glancing at his watch, a frown on his face, acting as if he were waiting for someone who was late. Where was she? This pointless chase of his. But it wasn't pointless. He had found out a lot about her. Found out that she was bored and restless and kind of sad, too. She had not smiled at all, had never looked amused or entertained by anything she had encountered. Seemed to be sleepwalking, killing time, hating to go home, maybe, the way he hated to go home.

He spotted her again as she pushed through a revolving door leading to the outside world. Hurrying, he side-stepped two elderly women, one of them with a cane, as he headed for the door. Pausing at a window next to the door, he saw her standing at the curb beneath the bus stop sign. For the first time, he *really* looked at her. Her blue plaid skirt fell in pleats and her pale blue sweater was fuzzy. She lifted her face as a gust of wind tousled her hair. Her hair was long enough to touch her shoulders, so black and shining that he thought it might squeak if he grabbed a bunch of it. Her features were delicate: small nose, high cheekbones, lips bare of lipstick. At that moment, she took a deep breath and her breasts rose in the sweater, straining against the fuzzy material. Looking away quickly, he felt dirty, like some kind of pervert. Yet, aroused at the same time. When he looked at her again, the bus was pulling up and she stepped toward it. A moment later, she had boarded the bus, the door closing behind her with a sigh. Watching the bus lurch away, he began to miss her. Which was ridiculous, of course, because he did not even know the girl.

The next day, she followed the same routine—hospital visit, then the bus to the Mall—and he trailed her from store to store as she drifted again, aimlessly. Because he was able to anticipate her movements, he didn't stay close to her, although he enjoyed being in her vicinity. Growing careless, he strolled by one of those multiple mirrors in Filene's and was stunned to see her reflection along with his own. Swiveling away, he almost collided with her, his right hand and her left hand touched briefly as they turned toward each other, so close that he smelled her perfume or cologne, something light and airy and springlike. The scent compounded his confusion and embarrassment. "Sorry," he muttered, aware of her mouth slightly open in surprise, her eyes startlingly blue, the blue of a child's crayon. Flustered, he stumbled away, cheeks flaming, disgusted with himself, swearing silently, damn it, damn it. Was his cover blown? His face known, his anonymity gone forever? He wondered as he left the store whether he should risk following her again. If he didn't, how would he ever meet her? The question surprised him. Why should he want to meet her? Shrugging the thought away, he headed for the parking garage, eager to get home, to seek the solace of the bottle.

Vowing to be extra careful, hoping she would not remember him, he followed her for the rest of the week. He refused to speculate about why he continued to observe her. Did not want to figure out his motives or reasons. All he knew was that she gave a purpose to his afternoons. He was pleased by the sight of her, the way she moved, her habit of touching her hair lightly now and then, her head tilted slightly.

On Friday, he knew that he would not see her again until the following Monday and he took more chances, shortening the distances between them. Then drew away, afraid of another encounter. Yet wanting an encounter.

Standing on the second level, he saw her come out of Miss Emily's Styles below. From this distance, she seemed forlorn, lonely, abandoned. An immense pity welled in him. *I told them she gave me the key,* Harry Flowers had said.

Getting on the escalator, he floated pleasantly downward. He glanced up as he prepared to step off the bottom step, saw the girl across the lobby looking hesitant, as if she were wondering what to do next. More than hesitant, sad.

That's when he tripped and fell. Did not really trip. The trick knee that had kept him out of basketball suddenly gave way as he stepped off the escalator, went all hollow on him, and he was propelled forward by the moving step, falling finally as if from a vast height, his nose brushing the tile floor, his elbow singing with pain as it struck the floor. Humiliated as he lay on the floor, wondering if his nose was broken, his arm aching as he raised his fingers to touch his nose—was it broken, bleeding?—he was relieved at the absence of blood. Disgusted, however, he did not raise his head, did not want to look up and see anybody, especially the girl, as he felt a crowd gathering, feet scuffling, heard murmurs and a clear child's voice saying: *He faw down.* No blood, nose intact. He opened his eyes and saw the small forest of legs around him and began to protest, as he muttered, "I'm all right, I'm all right, my trick knee," rising slowly by degrees, his nose numb, checking it with his hand, still no blood, his elbow still ringing with pain. Shamefaced, cheeks pounding, trying to ignore the faces around him, some sympathetic, others amused, old people, young people. He was surprised at the size of the crowd and looked to where he had seen the girl standing. She was gone. He breathed a sigh of thanks. Maybe she had not seen him fall so ingloriously, maybe had turned away before he went crashing to the floor.

"You okay?" A security guard in cop's uniform frowned as she regarded him, waving off the small crowd at the same time.

"Sure," Buddy said. "My trick knee." The words echoed in his mind as if he had said them a million times in the last few minutes. Maybe he had. "I'm fine," he assured the guard, wanting to get away. Walking away, in fact, even as he said the words, but carefully, not wanting to fall down again, second time in three minutes.

Responding to a sudden urgency for fresh air, grateful that his knee had righted itself and that he was barely limping, he headed for the nearest exit, aware of the eyes of the gathering at the escalator following him.

The air on the sidewalk was pleasantly bracing and he inhaled sharply, rubbing his elbow as if the pain could be eradicated that way. His nose was still numb but did not seem broken. He touched it tentatively.

"Does it hurt badly?"

He turned at the voice and saw the girl standing there, Jane Jerome, frowning, face tender with concern.

More blushing, more blood bouncing around in his cheeks. "It's okay," he said. "My trick knee." Damn it: *my trick knee* again. Shame suffused him once more as he realized she had seen him fall down so stupidly, after all.

"I fell down once, too," she offered. "My first day at Burnside after we moved there?" The curl of a question mark at the end of the sentence touched her words with beauty. "My heel broke and here I am, in a new school, right, and I start off by falling down in front of everybody. . . ."

Rubbing his elbow, listening to her voice, looking at the lips speaking those words, Buddy Walker fell instantly and irrevocably in love with Jane Jerome. At exactly 2:46 p.m. on a Friday afternoon in May at the Mall in downtown Wickburg.

She had had her crushes, her tragic loves, her worshipings from afar, but never anything like this. There had been unattainable Jeremy Madison, who played the lead in the school's abbreviated version of *Grease,* and made her feel weak when he passed her in the corridor and sent her heart into scary palpitations when his bare arm brushed her bare arm once in the cafeteria. He was one of the

unattainables among many: for instance, the entire Burnside High School football team, with whom she fell impos-
sibly in love one glorious Saturday afternoon as they
headed for the huddle, mysterious and glamorous in their
helmets, their faces glistening with sweat, a love that lasted
no more than the length of the game but inducing in her
body small sweet longings and strange intimate warmths.
Then Timmy Kearns. Her first and only date. The agony
and the ecstasy, like the title of that old movie. Both terrible and beautiful. She had adored him at a distance for
weeks and he finally asked her to the movies. Sweet ecstasy, head in a whirl, breathless, could not concentrate on
homework, got that awful C in math. Timmy Kearns had
turned out to be barely articulate, not shy or bashful but,
frankly, kind of stupid, kept scratching one particular spot
on his head. Scratched and scratched and scratched. Practically ignored her, too, although they sat together on the
bus, stood in line at the movies, sat next to each other in
the theater. He never looked her in the eyes. Not even
once. He never called her again, either. Which crushed her
beyond belief. Not because she had any *desire* to go out
with him again but because not being asked out on a *second* date was worse than no date at all, as if somehow you
had failed miserably. Patti and Leslie sympathized with her
—this was before the vandalism had changed everything—
but she still felt ashamed, especially when Timmy Kearns
who had been shooting her admiring glances for weeks
suddenly began to ignore her altogether, even when they
once met face-to-face carrying their trays of food in the
cafeteria, with practically the entire school watching.

So this thing—she had not yet given it a name—with
Buddy Walker was not like any of the other times she had
lost her heart. In fact, she did not feel as though she had
lost her heart but had found it at last. As if, until now, she

did not know she had a heart, not that kind of heart anyway. It began with empathy—she had shared his embarrassment when he fell down at the bottom of the escalator and saw the stricken look on his face even at that distance. She had left the scene because he looked familiar—she had seen him somewhere before, maybe at Burnside High —and it's always more embarrassing when you fall or do something like that in front of people you know, rather than strangers.

Then observing him outside as he rubbed his elbow, looking so dismal, as if he had been abandoned by his family and friends, good-looking but something sad and wistful about him, she had spoken to him spontaneously, surprising herself even as the words came out of her mouth. She had then made up that crazy story about her heel breaking. To make him feel better. Why should she have wanted to make this boy, this stranger, feel better? She did not know but a small curling inside her body responded to him, a leap in her veins when he looked at her, a look on his face that she could not interpret. The nearest she could come to describing that look was this: as if he were listening not only to her voice but to some sweet music coming from somewhere. And the somewhere was her.

She did not fall in love with him for another twenty minutes—it happened while they were chewing pizza with pepperoni at the Pizza Palace in the Mall—although she did not know it as love until later.

They became a couple, going steady. Walking along hand in hand. They loved to walk. On the sidewalks of Burnside and Wickburg, along the banks of the Grange River, through the lanes of Jedson Park, but most of all at the Mall. They were conscious of themselves as a couple, existing for themselves alone, wanting to be alone, yet aware of the people around them, wanting to be seen by others, glad to parade their love for all the world to observe.

She felt a pride of possession when she met fellows and girls she knew and managed to draw him closer to her. Once, they confronted Patti Amarelli and Leslie Cairns coming out of the Poster Store and Jane reveled in their envious glances, their undisguised awe as she and Buddy walked past. She could not keep herself from looking at him, stealing sly glances as they walked along. She loved the way he brushed back an errant lock of hair from his forehead or looked at her suddenly with a surprised expression on his face, as if he had just discovered her by his side and was delighted by the discovery. She could not stop touching him. Brushed against him, ran her hand along his arm, stroked that area at the base of his neck where his hairline stopped.

He became suddenly fastidious. Getting a haircut was now serious stuff, keeping his eye on the mirror as the barber snipped away, making certain every hair was in place. He had never used cologne, only simple Ivory soap, not even after-shave lotion. Now he used cologne after purchasing a bottle of Subtle at the perfume counter at Filene's. Sprayed the stuff on his cheeks and neck and arms. Wondering whether he had used too much or too little, he met Addy outside her room. She stopped, sniffed delicately, and shook her head.

"Buddy," she said, grinning, "you've got a girl friend."

Stunned, he said: "How do you know?"

"That smell can only mean one thing." Seeing his frown of embarrassment, she smiled indulgently: "I think it's great, Buddy. You don't have to go into details about it. But let me give you a helpful hint . . ."

The hint involved the cologne. "Don't spray the cologne directly on yourself," she advised. "Spray it into the air and then walk into it." Which she did as a demonstration. "That way you won't knock her down with the smell, it will be subtle like its name and creep up on her."

Grateful for her advice, he decided to tell her a bit about Jane. Not too much, afraid this rare thing he and Jane shared might be jinxed if he went on at length. Cautiously, he told Addy the bare essentials: her name, how they met. Addy did not push for details, listening attentively, a strange expression on her face, which he later realized was tenderness. "I'm so happy for you, Buddy," she said, touching his shoulder lightly.

Maybe Addy and I will become friends, after all, he thought, astonished at what love could do.

He became aware of the beauties of the world around him. Colors more brilliant, sunsets breathtaking, neon signs dazzling. Laughed easily at jokes, laughed at stuff that was not really *that* funny, like the stupid jokes Randy Pierce told at lunchtime in the cafeteria. Caught his reflection in a mirror sometimes and saw the idiotic grin on his face and didn't care.

Certain nights or afternoons, he and Jane did not see each other. Need to do homework, Jane said. And Buddy found himself doing homework, too. Sometimes they met in the Burnside Public Library and did their homework in the reading room, sitting side by side, and he managed to do the lessons despite the distraction of her presence. He felt older, more responsible, knowing that someday, if he was lucky, he would marry Jane Jerome, become her husband, a father—the prospect enough to take his breath away.

Jane passed lovely weightless days, floating almost, as if her feet barely touched the earth, capable of drifting off into the sky like a balloon and never be seen again, which would be awful because life on earth was so incredibly sweet. Spring exploded in a cascade of bird songs and flowers and she felt like a flower herself, opening, like the slow-motion flowers in a Disney movie. Ridiculous, of course, but not really. Walking along beside Buddy, she felt like a woman, yet irresistibly girlish at the same time. Wanted to flounce in dresses, feel silk next to her skin, nylon on her legs. Liked the sound of her clicking heels on the sidewalk or on the tile floor of the Mall. Delighted with herself, hugged herself a lot. She had a million secret places in her body that had not existed before she met Buddy and wanted him to explore them all, find them all out because she sensed that, in the finding out, there would be some kind of bliss involved. She often found that her eyes were brimming with tears and yet she was not crying. Instead of showers, she took long baths, trailed her fingertips along her flesh, held her breasts in her hands and they seemed to ache.

They could not get enough of each other, which made it necessary for them to have rules. Unspoken rules but rules all the same, declaring boundaries, how far they could go, by some mutual instinct. How long kisses should be, how far touching and caressing could proceed. Cupping her breast drove him wild, thick juices in his mouth, the threat of a sudden embarrassing eruption. But never both breasts and never inside her sweater. They embraced lovingly in a sweet tumble of bodies. Buddy never pushed beyond those silent limits, although one night he stiffened in the middle of the longest kiss they ever had, their mouths meshed, tongues wrapped around each other, his hand kneading her breast, and he fell away from her, shuddering, then became still, silent. She reached out in the dark—they were in the backseat of his mother's car—and

touched his cheek, felt moisture there, realized that tears
had spilled from his eyes. And took him in her arms, tenderly, delicately, loving him for those tears as she had
never loved him before.

Yet, there were mysteries about him that she could not
solve. He grew silent on occasion, deep in thought, un-
reachable, which panicked her, afraid that he would somehow slip out of her grasp or her life. She wanted him to
meet her parents but he always made some excuse for not
doing so. He seldom picked her up at her home, but when
he did he blew the horn and waited for her to come out of
the house. Most often, they met downtown, at the library,
at the Mall. Although this meant that she had to bus it to
downtown Wickburg, she didn't mind. He also had to bus it
from the other side of Wickburg and needed a transfer to
make the trip. She was vaguely disturbed but her accelerat-
ing heart, the small, sweet gasps of breath when he came
into sight, obliterated her misgivings.

She pondered whether she should tell him about the
trashing. Once or twice she brought up the subject. Subtly,
she thought. Said: "Some terrible things happen these
days, Buddy." She loved saying his name. "Like rape and
trashing."

A startled look on his face, he turned away from her.
Did not follow her lead. Changed the subject, in fact.
Pointed out something or other in the park.

Another time, she said: "Some people have no respect
for others."

"What do you mean?"

"Well, like other people's property. Wrecking it, trashing." That word again—*trashing.* Why couldn't she just
come out and tell him about what had happened? About
Karen in the hospital. Was she afraid that this would somehow alienate him, the way the trashing had come between

her and Patti and Leslie? But what she and Buddy shared
was different from those friendships, if they had been
friendships at all.

Why, then, didn't she take a chance? Did that hidden
part of him deter her? Or did it have to do with Harry
Flowers?

There, she had said his name. Ever since she met
Buddy, she had relegated Harry Flowers to the dim corners of her mind, refusing to think about him. Could not
allow herself to think of him. She knew that Harry Flowers
went to Wickburg Regional, where Buddy was also a student. Harry Flowers was a senior and Buddy, a junior. Did
Buddy know Harry Flowers? Did they nod to each other in
the cafeteria? Buddy used to play basketball—had they
been teammates? Stop it, stop it, she told herself. Stop
asking those questions. Wickburg Regional was a huge
high school, thousands of students, drawing them not only
from that city but the surrounding towns as well. It was
possible that they did not know each other, had not even
heard of each other.

Reveling in the glow of Buddy's love, she managed,
most of the time, to set aside her concerns about Harry
Flowers. Except for her visits to Karen in the hospital, she
could almost believe that the trashing had happened in
another place, another time of her life, a time that was
over and done with. Harry Flowers also belonged to that
time.

She also realized that the foul odor was gone from her
life along with the thought of Harry Flowers.

Thank God for Buddy Walker, she murmured one afternoon in the hospital chapel.

As if saying a prayer.

* * *

The first time Jane mentioned the word *trashing*, Buddy flinched, then turned away in self-defense, his thoughts racing wildly as he anticipated what her next words would be. He had to head her off, change the subject. Luckily, his eyes fastened on a funny-sad scene: a woman's shopping bag collapsed and all her groceries rolled haphazardly toward the gutter. He helped the woman retrieve the groceries and stood patiently with her, holding the soup cans, until her husband pulled up in his car.

Jane brought up the subject of trashing once or twice more and each time he was able to sidestep or change the subject. He had the distinct feeling that she wanted to talk about the trashing at her house. Why did she hesitate? Why didn't she simply tell him? Terrible thought: did she suspect that he had been involved? He shook his head in protest. How could she love him, let him hold her, kiss her, caress her, if she thought he had participated in the trashing, in hurting her sister? The possibility of having Jane find out that he was guilty, after all, was an ominous shadow in their relationship. The shadow that kept him drinking, even though his desire for booze had lessened since he had met her. He had to be more devious now, of course. Had to keep Jane from the knowledge of his drinking. He worried about his breath, wished that he could buy a guaranteed breath-freshener, not trusting Certs or Scope. He chewed all kinds of gum, which he hated, the taste too sweet and cloying. Sometimes held his breath or breathed through his nose when he was close to her. Felt her stiffen on occasion when they kissed, and wondered if she could taste the gin on his tongue. The simple thing, of course, would be to stop drinking altogether. But drinking these days enhanced the happiness that Jane had brought to him. The marvel of liquor: changing with his desires, magnifying the good things of his life. Drinking gently, not gulping frantically anymore but sipping slowly, bringing into focus the wonder of Jane and their love, allowing him visions of the two of them together through the coming years.

No more the intensity, the desperate quality of drinking but a different kind now, dreamlike, gentle.

Stepping through the revolving doors of Filene's one afternoon, they emerged on the sidewalk and met his mother. Stunned glances, time suspended for the fraction of a minute as they stared at each other. He stumbled through the introductions: "Jane . . . my mother . . . Mom . . . Jane Jerome . . ." His mother, elegant as usual, every hair in place although a windy day, paused, eyebrows raised in curiosity, glancing at him inquiringly as if to ask: How long has this been going on? And he realized, sadly, the chasm between their lives, how they did not connect anymore. She had not mentioned the retreat since that meeting in her bedroom. He had not asked her about it. Felt dismayed now.

"It's lovely to meet you," his mother said. He was proud of her stylish manner. Leaning confidentially toward Jane, she said: "Buddy has been so happy lately that I thought there must be something wonderful going on in his life. And now I see why . . ."

Which inflicted further guilt. He should have told her about Jane. Then thought: why hadn't she inquired if she saw how much I had changed? He saw that life was never simple.

Walking along later, whipped by the winds, Jane's hand tucked in his and both their hands in his jacket pocket, he thought about his mother and father—and love. How they had probably once been swept with the same

kind of love he and Jane shared. Did love change over the
years? Become diluted, pale? Or did it deepen? Or did it
become less equal? His father had fallen in love with
someone else. But not his mother. He knew how devas-
tated his life would become if Jane were to leave him. Is
that what had happened to his mother, abandoned by her
husband, the man she loved, the man who was supposed to
love her and keep on loving her through the years? Until
death do us part. And his father: he was in love now with
this woman, Fay, enough in love with her to leave his family. A terrible thing but—but did he feel toward that
woman, Fay, the way Buddy felt about Jane? Suppose he
had met Jane when he was involved with someone else
and . . .

"What's the matter, Buddy?" Jane asked, pressing
against him, warding off the wind, her hand still in his,
warm and moist.

"Nothing," he said, confused by his thoughts, by the
strange thing love could be.

"Your mother seems very nice," she said. "She's beautiful . . ."

Right. But my father still left her, he thought.

That night, he said to Jane: "I will love you forever."
Making a pledge, solemn, enduring.

He waited for her response, waited for her to say:

I will love you forever, too.

But she didn't speak, her head inclined, her hair
brushing his cheek, the scent of her shampoo radiant and
fresh.

He waited. Then said: "Jane?"

"Yes?"

"I said: I will love you forever."

She nestled closer to him.

"Will you love me forever, too?" Sad, because he had to ask.

She drew back, puzzled, a frown creasing her forehead. "Don't you know that by now?"

He hugged her to him, trembling inside, having just seen, as if in a light-bulb flash, how empty and meaningless his life would be without her.

Shuddering, he drew her to him, kissed her passionately, unendingly, until they drew away and she whispered tremulously: "Oh, Buddy."

The whole world in her voice as she spoke his name.

"When are we going to meet this mystery man of yours?" her father asked at the dinner table.

"He's not a mystery man, Dad," she replied. He's just . . . shy." Fumbling for the word *shy,* unable to find another word for Buddy's reluctance to meet her parents.

"Maybe there's no Buddy at all," Artie said. "Maybe he's a figment of her imagination, Dad." At times, there were flashes of the brat who had been her brother before the trashing. Although he still did not play his video games, he did not have nightmares anymore and had again joined the brat pack on the streets and sidewalks of the neighborhood.

"He's real, all right," Jane said, remembering his touch, the way he had tremblingly cupped her breast the night before. "Give us time . . ."

"He may be a very nice boy, Jane," her father said, an edge to his voice, "but I think we should meet him. I don't like the idea of having you dash out of the house and into his car . . ."

"His mother's car," she amended.

"I'm not talking about whose car," her father said, voice sharp now. "I'm talking about a boy you're spending a lot of time with, that you're all dreamy-eyed about, and we've never met him. He's never set foot into this house . . ."

"We're just trying to show you that we care about you," her mother said, gently, placatingly.

"Don't you trust me?" Jane asked.

"Of course we trust you, hon," her mother said. "But is it so unreasonable to want to meet this boy you think is so wonderful? Don't you want to share it all with us?"

Brushing her hair later in her room, she knew that her relationship with Buddy would remain incomplete until two things happened: telling him about the trashing and introducing him to her parents.

Both happened unexpectedly that same night.

She and Buddy had just stepped off the bus that brought them back to Burnside from Wickburg when they encountered her mother and father strolling along Main Street after seeing a movie at the Downtown Cinema. Flustered, embarrassed, but delighted, she managed the introductions and then stood silently proud as Buddy, very politely, shook their hands, murmuring "Pleased to meet you" a bit shyly, stammering endearingly. Looking at him through her parents' eyes, she was pleased at what she saw: a good-looking and polite young man, neat in his tan cords and brown sport shirt. Her pleasure increased when her father said: "Hope you'll drop around the house sometime," and Buddy answered: "Thank you, sir, I will."

Perhaps that meeting was the reason why, a few minutes later, Jane told him about the trashing as they sat on a park bench at the edge of Jedson Park, basking in the warmth and fragrance of the spring night. The words popped out of her mouth without plan or rehearsal.

"My house was trashed a while ago," she said. "These guys wrecked it. My sister is still in the hospital, in a coma.

She fell down the cellar stairs. Or was pushed . . ." Could say no more, her throat constricting.

His arm went around her shoulder, gripped her tightly. "I know," he said, voice hoarse as if his own throat were constricted.

"You knew all the time?" she asked, turned to him. "Why didn't you say something?"

"I didn't know how much it would hurt you to talk about it," he said. "I wanted you to do it in your own time."

"It was terrible, Buddy," she said, shuddering, relieved that the topic was out in the open and that he had not withdrawn from her. Her earlier reluctance to talk about the trashing was replaced now by a need to talk, to tell him what had happened from her point of view, not from what he had read in the newspaper or heard from other people. As she spoke he kept shaking his head, frowning, wincing sometimes as if her anguish were his own, as if he, too, had been damaged by the trashers. She had never loved him more than at this moment.

"Poor Buddy," she said, stroking his cheek. "Don't feel so bad. My family's fine now. The doctors are sure that Karen will come to soon. All the tests show that there is no brain damage." Actually, the doctors weren't sure at all—but she wanted to offer him consolation because he seemed so sad.

Later, when he left her at the steps of her house, he kissed her with a prolonged intensity that left her breathless, as if he would never kiss her again.

"I love you," she whispered as she slipped out of his arms. She had spoken those words to him a thousand times but never with such passion and fervor. "Thank you for being so wonderful . . ." Dashing into the house, she was exhilarated by the evening's events. But later, slipping on her pajamas, she wondered if she should have asked him about Harry Flowers.

While Buddy, at home, desperately drank himself into a stupor and then oblivion for the first time since he had met her.

They had just left the Pizza Palace at the Mall two days later when he spotted Harry Flowers stepping off the escalator. Buddy stiffened, looked around wildly for a place to hide although he knew there was no way to escape. He turned toward Jane, trying to block Harry's view of her and she leaned against him, misinterpreting his movement, thinking he wanted to get closer to her body. She looked up at him, smiling that self-satisfied smile he loved to see on her face. Taking her elbow, he steered her away from the escalator and she allowed herself to be navigated. He could not resist looking back over his shoulder, however, risking a quick glance to assure himself that Harry had come and gone without seeing them. The pizza with pepperoni became lead in his stomach when he saw Harry standing twenty-five feet away, a weird and evil smile on his face as he waved to Buddy.

Buddy did not wave back, did not acknowledge Harry's presence but maneuvered Jane around the corner, sick to his stomach suddenly.

That night, at home, he waited for the telephone to ring. He roamed restlessly around the house, looking out the windows, turning the television on, watching it awhile, then turning it off again. Harry Flowers: his nemesis, his downfall. After Jane had told him of the trashing on that park bench, he had been waiting for her to mention his name. His name had been in the newspaper. Jane had certainly read that story and saw it. Buddy waited, in fear that he would say: "Harry Flowers—he goes to Wickburg Re-

gional, too. Do you know him?" She had not mentioned
him but ever since, he had endured a special kind of tor
ture when they were together. He felt trapped, helpless
sensing that he was on the verge of losing Jane Jerome.

The telephone rang as he went into the bathroom. H
let it ring, standing motionless, hoped it would keep o
ringing and nobody would answer. Which was impossible
of course. Phone rings, someone answers.

"Buddy, it's for you," Addy called.

He picked up the phone in the living room, out o
earshot of Addy in her room and his mother going ove
household accounts in the den.

"Hey, Buddy, what's going on?" Harry asked. That sl
insinuating voice.

"Nothing," Buddy said. Maybe he had not seen hin
and Jane together, after all.

"Saw you at the Mall today, too bad we didn't have a
chance to talk . . ." Voice casual now, almost too casual
But at least no phony accent.

"Was that you? I thought it was you but wasn'
sure . . ."

"Oh, it was me all right, Buddy, but you seemed in a
hurry. Either that or you didn't want to talk to me righ
then . . ."

"Well, I *was* in sort of a hurry . . ." And let the sen
tence end, blowing air out of his mouth.

"You were with a girl, Buddy. You keeping secret
from Harry? Got a girl friend and haven't told Harry abou
it?"

"She's not my girl," Buddy said. "Just a girl I know
We have a pizza together once in a while. I think we wen
to a movie once."

"You *think* you went to a movie? Aren't you sure

Buddy? Is your memory that bad? I mean, did you go to a movie with this girl or didn't you?"

"Yeah, that's right, we did go to a movie. I mean, it wasn't really a date . . ."

How can I get out of this stupid conversation?

"Who is she, Buddy? Anybody at school? Anybody I know?"

"No, you wouldn't know her."

"Why wouldn't I know her? I mean, I know a lot of people, Buddy, and you don't know everybody I know, do you? So how do you know I wouldn't know her?"

Jesus, Buddy thought, perspiration gathering in his armpits, his palms, his crotch, everywhere.

"Well, she's new in town. So I figured you wouldn't know her. I mean, she doesn't know many people here and she doesn't go to Wickburg Regional . . ."

"Where does she go then?"

Buddy's hand was so slippery with sweat that the telephone almost slid from his grasp.

"I don't know."

"You don't know? Let me get this straight. You're going out with this girl, right, you eat pizza with her, right, you go to the movies with her and you don't know where she goes to school?"

"She doesn't like to talk about it. About school, I mean. She's having problems transferring from out of town and would prefer not to discuss it."

Buddy's mind was racing so fast, to lie, to fabricate, that he felt dizzy.

"Poor kid," Harry said, and Buddy tried to pin down whether Harry's sympathy was real or synthetic. "Know what, Buddy? I just caught a glimpse of her. I mean, you were blocking my view of her, for crissakes. But she looked familiar. I don't know. I've been trying to place her ever

since. Something about her. I've seen her before somewhere . . ."

"Is that right?" Could Harry hear the hollowness in his
voice?

"Yes, it's one of those things. You know, like a name
on the tip of your tongue and you can't quite remember . . ."

"Sure, I know what you mean." Was Harry toying with
him, teasing him?

"Listen, what is her name, anyway? Maybe that will
solve my memory problem . . ."

"Her name?"

"Yes, you know. What's on her birth certificate. What
she signs on her theme papers at school, what she puts
down at the end of her letters."

He knows, of course, he knew all along.

Reckless suddenly, figuring he had nothing whatever
to lose, he said: "Guess, Harry."

"Guess what?"

"Guess her name. You're good at games. Go ahead,
guess."

Let him say her name, if he knows it. I'm not saying it.

"Give me a clue, then."

"Like what?"

"Like her initials. The initial of her first name."

"Nope, you've got to guess the whole name."

Big pause. Buddy almost smiled. Harry liked cat-and-
mouse stuff and he was being given a taste of it.

Harry sighed. "This is going to be hard. I mean, there
are twenty-six letters in the alphabet and her name has to
start with only one of them. I'll tell you what, Buddy. I'll
have to think about it. I'll have to give it some time. Let me
think about it tonight and I'll call tomorrow and give you
my guesses. Okay?"

"Okay," Buddy said, trying to disguise the relief in his voice.

"But you know what might be even better?"

"What's that, Harry?"

"Maybe I should call up Jane Jerome and ask her about that fellow I saw her with this afternoon at the Mall. Think she'd make me guess?"

Harry hung up almost before the word *guess* was out of his mouth and Buddy Walker stood there, the dial tone like a small explosion in his ear.

Harry did not call back for two days and Buddy became anxious. Knowing Harry, familiar with his tricks and techniques, he wondered whether he was planning one of his exploits, as he playfully called them. On the third day, he decided to confront Harry and waited for him at the doorway to the school cafeteria before lunch break.

Harry was alone, for which Buddy was grateful. He stepped in front of him, planted himself in front of him, in fact, barring his entry into the cafeteria.

"I want to talk to you," Buddy said.

"I'm really starved, Buddy," Harry said. "I hear they're having meat loaf. You know how I love meat loaf. And I hate to talk while I'm eating . . ."

The smirk on Harry's face, his cool appraising eyes, the what-the-hell way he stood—all of this was irritating but Buddy had to accept it.

"This'll only take a minute," Buddy said. He had seen Harry talking a mile a minute many times while eating but knew that this was another pretense, another game he enjoyed playing.

Harry lifted his shoulders in surrender, indicating his patience with friends.

"Okay, Harry, so the girl is Jane Jerome."

Harry raised his nose to the air. "That meat loaf smells delicious." Buddy could detect no aroma at all in the air, only the stale smell of the corridor itself. "Why were you avoiding me at the Mall, Buddy? Why didn't you at least wave? Maybe even introduce me?"

Aghast, Buddy said: "For crissakes, Harry, you were in court for wrecking her house. Your name was in the newspaper. And you wanted to be introduced?" Buddy bowed in exaggerated fashion. "Hey, there, Jane Jerome, let me introduce Harry Flowers. Name sound familiar? He's the guy who trashed your house . . ."

Harry smiled his lazy smile. "And then I would say: And how about Buddy Walker here? Has he mentioned that he was with me when we trashed the house and took special pains with your bedroom?" Frowning at Buddy: "Did you or didn't you piss on her wall? Or did you just vomit on the carpet?"

Speechless, Buddy turned away, all appetite gone, actually smelling the meat loaf wafting from the cafeteria but finding it repugnant. When he turned back to Harry, his face was only inches away, Harry leaning in to him.

"What the hell are you doing with her?" Harry asked. "You some kind of madman? Looking for trouble?" Then relenting a bit, withdrawing: "How did all this get started anyway?"

"I called her up. To tell her I was sorry."

"And she decided to go out with you?" Disbelief in his voice.

"No, she doesn't know it was me who called. But when I heard her voice on the telephone . . ." And he told Harry, who kept sniffing the air for aromas of meat loaf, about following her in the Mall and falling down and the rest of it.

"I love her, Harry. And she loves me," he finished, lamely.

"But what happens when she finds out, Buddy? What happens then?" He seemed sincere, now, as if he really cared.

"She won't find out," Buddy said, his words more convincing than his feelings.

"Of course she will," Harry said, "Wickburg's a small place and Burnside is even smaller. Is her sister still in the hospital? Still in a coma?"

Buddy nodded, trapped, knowing what question Harry was going to ask before he asked it, because he had asked himself that question a thousand times. And Harry asked it:

"What happens when she comes out of the coma? When Jane Jerome says, 'Karen, I'd like you to meet my boyfriend, the guy I love.' And she looks at you and remembers that night?"

"I'm not sure if she saw me that night," he said. "I was upstairs when she came in the house."

"You're in a no-win situation, Buddy," he said. "Sooner or later, Jane Jerome's going to find out you were in the house that night whether her sister remembers you or not. You picked the wrong girl to fall in love with. The wrong girl and the wrong time . . ."

"She's worth the chance, Harry," he said.

Harry stretched his arms, flexed his shoulders. "Ah, smell that meat loaf," he said, sniffing the air again. "Time to indulge the appetite."

"You go ahead, I'm not hungry," Buddy said. Even if he had been hungry, he would not have wanted Harry Flowers's company during lunch.

As Harry walked away, he shot Buddy a glance over his shoulder.

"Another thing you should worry about, Buddy," he said. "Suppose somebody decides to tell Jane Jerome all about you and what you did to her room?"

He left Buddy standing there, like a target on a shooting range with no place to hide.

The whiteness of the ceiling woke her up.

But that was silly.

Ceilings, not even white ones, didn't wake people up. What did then?

She didn't know. Noise, alarm clocks, Mom calling from downstairs: "Get going, Karen, you'll be late for school." Those things woke you up.

But not ceilings.

Besides, she was looking down at the ceiling and ceilings should be *up* not down.

She closed her eyes, demolishing the ceiling, but the darkness of her closed lids threatened to engulf her, eat her up, and she opened her eyes again.

The ceiling was still white but this time it was above her where it should be and she saw a crack in the ceiling, like a small streak of lightning caught forever in white.

She blinked her eyes rapidly, testing them, to see if they worked, which was also silly but somehow necessary. She tried to move. Or rather she thought about moving, again testing, although she couldn't figure out why she should be testing herself like this. And why should she be here?

But where was *here*?

That's when the panic hit, like a wave engulfing her, swinging her up and over so that she felt her body lifting, straining at the sheet but more than the sheet, something pulling at her arm, her arm imprisoned, held fast, tied to a

terrible something next to the bed, from which came a hum
or a blip, she wasn't sure which.

She knew suddenly with the force of a door slamming
in her face that she was in a hospital and she had an image
of stairs tumbling around her, up and down, but the memory and the panic were like shivers now, even her blood
seemed to be shivering like icy worms that had been disturbed under her flesh and she was about to scream when
she plunged into darkness and everything was wiped away
like crazy drawings on a blackboard.

Jane found out about Buddy's drinking in the lobby of
the Wickburg Cinema when a half-pint bottle of gin
dropped out of his jacket pocket as he stooped to pick up
one of her pearl earrings that had fallen to the floor.

Later, Buddy realized he had been stupid to have carried the bottle while on a date with Jane. Before leaving
home, he had, on impulse, slipped the bottle into his jacket
pocket. Just in case. In case of what? He didn't know. But
he was jumpy. Had to be prepared. Prepared for what? For
anything. In case. In case of what? In case Karen suddenly
recovered and Jane wanted to take him to the hospital to
meet her. In case Harry double-crossed him, made a phone
call to Jane, for instance. In case, for crissakes.

Jane was stunned when she saw the bottle tumble out
of his jacket and shatter on the lobby floor. She knew immediately that it was some kind of liquor even though it
was as clear as water as it spread across the polished tile.

Still she asked:

"What's that?"

Buddy, speechless, on one knee, stared at the mess of
broken glass and spreading gin.

"Bud . . . dee," she said, drawing out his name.
"What were you doing with that bottle in your pocket?"

Conscious now of the people streaming by, looking at them
curiously, someone giggling, someone else snickering.

"I . . ." That was all Buddy could utter, not wanting
to look at Jane, and not wanting to look at the mess either,
and wondering what the hell he was supposed to do with it.
He began to pick up the shards of glass, handling them
gingerly to avoid cutting himself and then looked around
for a waste container, couldn't see one through the legs of
people passing by. He looked up, dreading to see the look
on her face, the look that would match the horror of her
voice. But she was gone.

Standing by his mother's car in the parking lot, Jane
felt as though the pieces of a puzzle had come together to
form a picture, not a really clear picture but a picture anyway. Of Buddy as a drinker, maybe an alcoholic. She
wasn't sure about any of that. Yet, there had been clues
that she had ignored simply because they had not made
any sense in relation to the Buddy she knew and loved.
The smell on his breath sometimes, what she thought was
some kind of medicine. His incessant chewing of gum or
Life Savers after he had admitted once that he hated gum
and Life Savers. His slurred speech on occasion. For a
time, she actually thought he had a speech defect that he
was trying to cover up. All unconnected in her mind, her
suspicions coming and going so swiftly that she had barely
acknowledged them. Waiting for him now, the crowd thin-
ning out, thankful that he had parked under a floodlight,
she winced as she thought of him kneeling on the floor of
that lobby, his head hanging down, like the first time she
had seen him at the Mall. God, how she loved him. But
that love was now a lonely aching that had found its way
into every crevice of her body.

She saw him coming slowly across the parking lot,
head down, like a little boy going home to be punished.

Tenderness entered her aching and brought tears to her
eyes.

"Oh, Buddy, poor Buddy," she murmured, a bit of pity
mixed with the tenderness. Maybe she had leaped to wrong
conclusions, maybe she had exaggerated those clues. All
she wanted to do was to gather him into her arms and kiss
away all the bad things in their lives.

The argument went on for more than an hour in the
car in the parking lot, the theater crowd long gone, the
night turning chilly and the wind kicking stray bits of paper
across the pavement.

"But it's not a problem," Buddy insisted. "I drink because I like to drink. And if I stop drinking, then that's
admitting that it was a problem. See what I mean?" He was
amazed at his sharpness, how he could be so logical and
persuasive, although doubt remained on Jane's face. And a
distant look in her eyes, as if she were contemplating
things she could not articulate.

"But it's not natural, Buddy," she said, trying to remain calm and keep her voice reasonable, disguising the
panic that had her in its thrall. "You're in high school. You
should not be drinking at all. All right, maybe at a party or
something. But not as much as you do. . . ."

He frowned, wondering what she would think if she
knew how much he actually drank. He had told her that he
liked a drink now and then while doing his homework and
to relax after school. "Not very much," he had said.

"How much is not very much?"

His thoughts scurried. "Oh, maybe a pint every few
days." Knowing he had to walk a delicate line here, not
saying too much or too little. When he saw her face stiffen,
he knew he had gone too far. And tried to amend it: "I
never really count. I don't even think it's that much . . ."

Her questions were unending. Where do you buy the stuff? How can you buy it when you're not old enough? Who sells it to you?

He answered guardedly, telling her the truth but shading it. Did not tell her about the times he could not connect with Crumbs and lurked in the park with the bums, feeling like a bum himself. Did not tell her about the hangovers in the morning when he stumbled his way to school, waiting to get to his locker where he had stashed a bottle. Did not tell her that right now, this minute as they were talking, as he was insisting that he drank because he liked it and could give it up any time, he was desperate for a drink, he was dying for the sweet balm of the booze.

"Why did you take that bottle to the movies tonight?" she asked, honestly curious.

He lifted his shoulders in a weary shrug. Could not tell her the truth and could not think of a lie. He hated the word *lie. Excuse* was a better word. He could not think of an excuse that she would accept.

"When you went to the john once, was that so you could have a drink from the bottle?" She remembered how he had returned chewing Dentyne furiously.

"No," he said. Lying. He was a liar.

"You're lying," she said, her voice flat with accusation and regret.

He turned to look at her and saw her as the enemy. The girl he loved but still an enemy. Her eyes flashing with anger and something else beside the anger. Sadness maybe.

"Okay, I lied because I didn't want you to feel bad," he said.

"But why did you have to go and have a drink of whiskey during the movie?"

"It's not whiskey. It's gin."

"It's liquor," she said.

"Because it makes me feel better," he said, blurting out the truth at last. "Because the world is sometimes a rotten place and it takes away the rotten things . . ." The rotten things he had done—like the trashing.

"How about me?" she said. "How about us? How can you say the world is rotten if we have each other?"

Tears flooded her eyes, more than tears. Sobs, her shoulders heaving, her body shuddering, uncontrolled. She had not cried like this since she was a baby, maybe never had cried like this. And then she was in his arms, encircled by him and he was murmuring against her cheek as she clutched him.

"I love you, Jane. You're not part of the rotten world —you're the reason why I'm happy. You make the rotten things go away . . ."

Like the gin, she thought. I'm like liquor to him.

His love for her was a sudden rushing through his body and he saw what a wretched lonely thing his life would be without her. Worse than being without the booze. He thought of the emptiness of the days ahead if he should lose her. He started to cry, his tears joining hers as their cheeks met. "I love you, Jane," he said, his voice strangled, unrecognizable to himself. "I love you more than drinking."

Stifling her own sobs, moved beyond words at the sight of Buddy crying, his mouth crooked, his nose running, his hair disheveled, she waited for him to say the words she longed so achingly to hear. And he said them:

"I'll stop drinking, Jane. I promise that I won't drink anymore . . ."

He spent three drinkless days without any trouble at all, his desire for liquor obliterated by this second chance with Jane. Yet, he admitted in a small part of his mind that there had to be a different solution. The prospect of living the remainder of his life without having another drink was impossible to contemplate. In his panic and desperation that night in the car, those words *I won't drink anymore* were the final weapons he had used to keep from losing her and he believed them utterly when he spoke them.

During those three days, wistfulness descended upon him like a sad mist, although he did not have any thirst for a drink or longing for its effects. However, a certain light seemed to have dimmed in his life, as if the sun were still shining but through dark clouds. Stop with the self-pity, he told himself. Jane is your sunshine, like that old song says.

Since he had started drinking seriously a few months before, he had become aware of articles on alcoholism and sometimes read them. Then he stopped reading them. He refused to take the tests the articles often contained, like, on the seven or eight or nine signs of alcoholism. He had flunked too many tests in school, he didn't need to flunk any on liquor. But he became aware of the AA slogans and in those first few days of his promise, he made use of them, especially *One Day at a Time* and *Easy Does It.* He cut himself off from thoughts of the future. He concentrated instead on today not tomorrow, or next week. The trick seemed to work, at least for the time being.

Another trick: the bottle of gin in the garage, which he had stashed away before the promise and was untouched. He had always tried to keep an extra bottle on hand, remembering the times of panic when he didn't have any liquor in the house or no money or on Sunday when the stores were closed. (Once he raided his father's liquor cabinet but had been disappointed to find one lonely bottle of whiskey, almost empty so that he could risk only a quick brief gulp.) As a result, he had tried to keep a spare on hand and that spare remained at this moment in the garage. Three days since he had had a drink, three days of bliss with Jane—she had never been so tender, so loving, allowing him the night before to remove her blouse and bra and kiss her breasts. Let the bottle stay untouched, he said to himself that afternoon of the third day as he plunged into his homework in his room, the volume on his CD turned up so high, the walls seem to buckle with the assault of heavy metal.

But on the fourth day, depression set in. The blues. A rotten test in English Lit. simply because he hadn't read the chapter. Came face-to-face with Harry Flowers on three occasions and Harry's face had been like a stone wall, unreadable, cold. Diarrhea this morning, upset stomach. Jane had remained at school this afternoon, trying out for the chorus. Rain slanted against the window. A perfect setup, he thought, for the booze but I'm not buying. Despite the blues, the down feeling, the grayness of things. He wandered into his parents' bedroom. Saw the unmade bed. An unmade bed would have been impossible when his father was still here in the house. The sadness of the tousled blankets, the pillow rumpled and punched in, brought tears to his eyes. His mother did not seem to care anymore. She had not mentioned going on retreat again and he had neglected to ask her if she had changed her mind. He should take more interest in his mother, Addy, and what was happening in all their lives. More reasons for the blues.

He wandered into the garage strictly out of curiosity, to see if the bottle was still there, knowing that he could not always trust his memory these days. He certainly would not take a drink from the bottle, not at this stage of events. Whistling softly, he reached under the usual pile of debris and found the bottle in its brown paper bag. Took it out and looked at it. Still sealed. *Think of Jane. And one day at*

a time. He slipped the bottle back into the bag and returned it to the hiding place. Then stood there, feeling sad.
More than sad. Down, depressed, the pits. Indecisive.

The telephone rang, far away, in the house. Let it ring.
He thought of that bottle in the bag, so close. What if he
only took a sip or two, enough to soothe the edges, smooth
out the rough spots? The ringing continued. *First, answer
the phone. Then we'll see.*

He went into the house, fearful now that he wouldn't
reach the phone in time, that whoever was on the other
end of the line would hang up before he reached it. But it
still rang. When he picked up the receiver, he was astonished to hear his father's voice:

"Buddy, how are you?"

Without waiting for an answer, his father went on:
"I'm calling to see if we might get together."

All thoughts of the bottle in the garage vanished as
Buddy heard himself saying: "Great, Dad. Any time you
say. Morning, noon, or night."

One minute not there.

The next minute there.

That was the way she reached consciousness the second time. She did not know precisely how or when, knew
only that she was suddenly present and alive on the planet
earth, staring up at the ceiling. The ceiling had a crack in it
that was strangely familiar. She directed her attention away
from the ceiling to the rest of the room and knew instantly
she was in a hospital, and that she had been here for a long
time. She did not know *how* she knew but was certain of
her knowledge, as if she had absorbed it into her system
the way she absorbed the liquid seeping into her arm from
the bottle suspended above her at the side of the bed. She
listened to the small beeping sound and the hum of a

nearby machine and closed her eyes, content to lie dreamily, hazily in the bed.

Sounds leaped in her ears, magnified, as if her ears were actually speakers in some gigantic stereo system. Footsteps padded by, a door closed, then a muffled cry, all the sounds sweet, as if she had been deaf a long time and could suddenly hear. A small scratching sound—she listened intently, trying to drown out the other noises. More than a scratching sound, a kind of whistle—of course, a bird, a robin outside her window, louder than a robin, a blue jay, possibly.

Footsteps joined the small screeching of the blue jay and she looked toward the door as a nurse entered the room. Jolly face, apple cheeks, glasses perched on her nose, and a smile of happy surprise when she saw Karen awake.

Hello, Karen wanted to say. I'm Karen Jerome and I don't know where I've been but I'm back now.

When she tried to speak, the words would not form on her lips and her mouth worked futilely, as if it belonged to somebody else.

Careening. That was the word Jane used to describe the car as her father drove to the hospital. Ordinarily, her father was the safest of drivers, to the point of making everyone crazy. He always slowed down even as he approached a green traffic light, afraid it would turn to yellow if he continued into an intersection. He obeyed all the traffic rules and had never received a ticket, even for overtime parking.

But now he drove with what only could be called abandon through Burnside streets, taking a corner perilously, the engine protesting and the wheels squealing as if some demented teenager were at the wheel. To her father, every teenager at the wheel of a car was demented.

The speed with which they were driving was unnecessary because the hospital was only a few blocks away from their house. But her father seemed to enjoy speeding while her mother clamped her hand to her head as if she were holding an invisible hat, and Jane and Artie looked at each other with delight.

For the first time in his life, her father parked in a No Parking space directly in front of the hospital steps and almost leaped out of the door, running around the front of the car, waiting for the rest of the family to join him.

It was difficult to believe that in a few moments, they would see Karen awake again, hear her speak, sit up in bed maybe or even leave it.

"Let's go," her father called impatiently over his shoulder, a lovely impatience as he led them up the steps to the hospital door.

Karen studied her mother and father and Jane and Artie. Saw them clearly and sharply, no fuzz at all at the edges of her vision. The fuzz had been there earlier when she tried to focus on distant spots of the room. They were staring anxiously at her, which made her sad. But something else besides anxious. Expectant. The word was strange to Karen—but that was it. They looked as if they expected something to happen. And for a moment Karen was annoyed. Wasn't it enough that she was back, had returned from—she wasn't sure where but it had been far far away—anyway, what did they expect her to do? Jump up and sing and dance? She scolded herself. She should be happy to be back after all those weeks in the darkness.

She smiled at her family. Or at least she formed what she hoped was a smile, arranging her lips the way she would arrange flowers in a bouquet. Which was a crazy thought, of course. But everything was crazy. Being here in the hospital, all those weeks of nothing, not even sleep—it had not felt like sleep, although she could not express in words what being in a coma felt like.

They were still staring at her. Her father in his usual suit and striped tie, staring. Her mother, hair a bit askew and staring. Jane in a new blue sweater Karen had never seen before, staring. And Artie, video-mad Artie with his Nintendos, also staring. All of it weird.

She wanted to talk to them. Explain. Explain that she was fine, despite what the doctor had told her: she had fallen down the stairs at home. She could not remember falling down the stairs. She remembered something but wasn't sure what. She remembered shadows. She remembered being afraid like when she was a little girl and woke up in the middle of the night, resenting Jane who always fell asleep instantly and never woke up in the night afraid. She did not remember falling down the stairs. Do you remember anything else? the doctor had asked. She could not remember the doctor's name. He had told her his name but she could not remember it. She wanted to remember it because the doctor was very nice. He answered her questions before she asked him. Actually, she was unable to ask the questions. For some stupid reason, she could not speak. She had forgotten how to talk. Which was ridiculous, of course. But the doctor said that she had come a long way—*progressed* was the word he used—and that time would take care of things, don't worry. Then told her, without her having to ask, what had happened. How she had fallen down the stairs. But she knew that it was not that simple. There was something else, just beyond the horizon of her memory. A shadow, more than one shadow, and the shadows had faces. She did not know whose faces.

Please, she thought, looking at her family, don't look at me like that. Like I'm behind a glass wall and you can't touch me. When they first came into the room, they had gathered around the bed, hugging and kissing and saying sweet words and she had basked in those words, letting herself be carried in the caresses and the murmurs. Then tried to work her mouth but nothing came out. *Hey, everybody, look, I've forgotten how to speak.* Funny, but not funny at all.

She did not mind not being able to speak. Time will take care of it, the doctor whose name she could not remember had said. What made her feel sad was that she could not tell her mother and father not to worry. I'm all right. I feel fine. Later, when she was stronger, she would write them notes.

Then for some reason, she began to cry.

Hated herself for crying.

For what her crying did to them.

Because they started crying, too. Her mother, her father, and Jane and Artie. Everybody crying.

Thank God the doctor entered the room at that moment. The doctor always looked tired. Long thin tired face. But then he smiled and didn't look tired anymore. Made you feel good. And now he smiled at her family and this made her feel good, too.

She closed her eyes, afraid for just a moment that she might plunge into that coma again but instead let herself drift into the sweet, sweet, sweetness of sleep.

Buddy met his father for lunch at one of those brass-and-fern restaurants in downtown Wickburg. His father's eyes were bloodshot. His face drawn, as if he were not getting enough sleep.

"You look great," his father said, voice hearty but hoarse.

"You look great, too, Dad," Buddy lied, flooded with sudden affection for his father. He looked so . . . sad. Buddy was suddenly willing to forgive him here and now for whatever he had done to break up the family.

After the waiter brought the menu, his father ordered a martini, dry. Turning to Buddy: "Martinis have gone out of style these days. But I'm old-fashioned, I guess."

His father had two martinis before lunch and two glasses of white wine with the meal. Buddy drank three Cokes, Classic. Managed to eat the hamburger and french fries although his appetite was absent. Answered his father's questions about school, his marks, Addy. Waited for him to ask about his mother, his father's wife—they weren't yet divorced, for crying out loud—but waited in vain. He was tempted to tell him about Jane but held back for some reason, not certain why. He watched his father sipping the wine and sighing after each sip as if it were some rare vintage. He was surprised to find that he was not dying for a drink, as if through some kind of magic the booze his father consumed was somehow being transfused into himself, taking away his own desire.

His father ate his small steak without enthusiasm, as if only marking time between sips of wine, smacking his lips a bit after each sip, holding the glass up once and looking at it appreciatively.

While Buddy waited. And wondered what he was waiting for. Then knew he was waiting for his father to get to the point, to divulge the purpose of the lunch. A wild hope rose. Was his father returning home? Was he building up to a big announcement?

The waiter removed their plates. Dessert menu? Both

shook their heads and then his father said: "Wait, maybe another martini. Want another Coke?" his father asked.

As Buddy held up his half-filled glass, he studied his father more closely than ever before, trying to see him as a stranger would see him. The word that leaped into his mind was: *ruin*. As if his father's face, which he'd remembered as pink and lean and handsome, had fallen on hard times. Small veins were visible in his nose and cheeks, as if there had been tiny explosions under the surface of his flesh. More flesh had gathered under his eyes. His eyes were not only bloodshot but sore-looking, as if he'd been staring at the sun too long.

"You happy, Dad?" Buddy asked, the question startling him even as he spoke the words.

"What kind of question is that, Buddy?" he said, obviously taken by surprise.

"I just wondered." *You don't look happy.*

"I don't know whether we're meant to be happy or sad all the time," his father said. "I mean, it's like taking your temperature just to see if you have a fever when there's no need for it."

He's talking in circles, Buddy thought. Or maybe he's right. Why do we always have to be either happy or sad? Why not just *be*?

"Don't you want to know how Mom is?" he asked, needing to lash out, say something, *do* something.

"I know how she is, Buddy," he answered, sighing wearily. "Miserable. And I'm the one who made her miserable. Guess I'm miserable, too, sometimes."

"Why, Dad? Why did all of this happen to make everybody so miserable?"

His father glanced around the room, caught the waiter's eyes and signaled for this drink, mouthing the word *martini*. "Things happen," he said, settling back in his chair. "We don't go looking for things to happen but they do."

Buddy plunged: "Are you ever coming back home, Dad?" Not too big a plunge: if his father was miserable sometimes, maybe he wanted to come home.

Big silence. His father fingered the empty glass, looked around the room again. "Where's that waiter?" he asked, irritated, drumming the table.

With sudden clarity, Buddy saw that his father needed another martini more than he needed to answer Buddy's question. Or needed that drink before answering. He wondered about that old saying: like father, like son. Would he grow up to be like his father, still drinking, his face filled with the tiny flowers? Would he someday make Jane miserable and become miserable himself?

Giving up his search for the waiter, his father looked at him directly. "No, Buddy. I'm not coming back. I don't even think your mother wants me back or would take me back. It's like a broken window, Buddy, the glass shattered. You can't fix it. You get a new window . . ."

These are not windows, Dad.

That's what Buddy wanted to say but he remained silent as he saw his father still angling to see if the waiter was approaching with his drink, fingering the empty wineglass, glancing into it to see if there might be a drop or two left then actually, *actually* raised it to his lips to drain away whatever dregs might be left.

He could not wait for this terrible luncheon to end.

Jane called Buddy from the pay telephone in the lobby of the hospital, eager to share the good news of Karen's recovery. The telephone rang and rang.

Karen wasn't completely recovered, of course. She had regained consciousness, had suffered no loss of locomotion (the doctor's word) and was functioning normally (more doctor words) except for her inability to speak. Which was probably not physically originated (the psychiatrist's words now) but a temporary condition. Seven, eight rings. She hoped Buddy's lunch with his father went well. He had been excited about the invitation, like a little boy going to the circus with his daddy.

She was about to hang up when he answered. "Hello," his voice dim, subdued. Was something wrong?

"Buddy," she said. "How was lunch?" *Please say that lunch was fine, that you and your father had a good time.*

"Okay," he said, the word lacking in enthusiasm. Had the lunch gone wrong? She would have to deal with that later.

"Karen is out of her coma," she said, unable to suppress her excitement. "I'm calling from the hospital—she's going to be all right. . . ."

Silence from Buddy. She was a bit angry that the lunch had not gone well and was spoiling her news about Karen.

"That's great," he said, the words booming with enthusiasm across the wires. Was he playacting? He sounded *too* enthusiastic, now, his voice, like, too loud, too high. "You must be happy. I mean, your parents must be walking on air."

His voice still sounded fake. It must have been a terrible lunch. "There's only one thing wrong," she said, "She can't speak. The doctor says it's psychological. Listen, can we get together somewhere? Can you come over to Burnside? We can get a Coke or something and you can tell me all about lunch with your father and I'll tell you all about Karen. . . ."

"Sure, good," he said, and his voice was again normal, the voice of the Buddy she knew and loved.

"Give me fifteen minutes and I'll be there," he said.

After all this time, the sound of his voice still thrilled her.

The Avenger could not believe his eyes.

There she was, Jane Jerome, his Jane, with one of the trashers. Standing beside him on the sidewalk, holding his hand. Looking up at the trasher as if nobody else in the world existed. Looking up at him with—what?—a tender expression on her face. A look of love.

The Avenger stood still. Stood still on the outside, that is. Inside, he was all movement and turmoil, his blood surging through his veins, his temples throbbing, his face growing hot, hotter, until he was afraid his cheeks would explode and pieces of his flesh would fly through the air and splatter the sides of buildings. At the same time he needed to go to the bathroom, desperately, afraid he would have an accident right here on Main Street in front of Dupont's Drug Store. But the urge to go to the bathroom was replaced by the need to hide as they began crossing the street, heading in his direction. He had to get away, out of their sight. Spinning completely around, he searched for ways of escape, and saw the alley between Dupont's and Burnside Video. He hurried into the alley, and hugged the wall. Saw Jane and the trasher pass by, still holding hands. He waited a moment, surrounded by the smell of garbage from a nearby barrel. Did not breathe, did not want to inhale the smell of garbage, did not want to bring the smell inside his body.

After a while, he stepped out of the alley. Did not see them anywhere. He walked slowly toward the video store, looked in the window, using his hand as a visor. Saw them. Jane and the trasher. Was he really the trasher? He squinted, studying the boy. Yes, he was one of them, all right. No doubt at all. The images of the trashers were burned into his mind like with a branding iron. This trasher was not the one with the hammer and not the fat one who screamed loudest of all and not the thin ratty-looking one. But one of them. Good-looking but evil just the same. You can't judge a book by its cover, his mother always said.

Did Jane know that he was one of the trashers? Maybe she didn't know. Maybe he was fooling her. Or maybe she knew and didn't care. He remembered something about a key, a rumor in the neighborhood that Jane had given the trashers the key to her house. He had not believed that for a minute. Now he wasn't sure. Maybe she *had* given the key to one of the trashers, maybe to this boy in the store with her. At that moment, he saw the boy join her in one of the aisles. He saw Jane reach up and draw the boy into her arms. He saw her wrap her arms around him, saw her mashing her mouth against his, saw her tongue go into the trasher's mouth. Revolted, grimacing, he could not take his eyes from them. How could she do such a thing? She should have known when she touched him—with her tongue! her tongue!—that he was one of the trashers. Even if he wasn't a trasher, she should not be kissing him like that, like some animal.

It was at that moment that The Avenger began to hate Jane Jerome, hate her worse than even the trashers. She was not a nice person. No nice person would do what she was doing in that store with her mouth, her tongue. To a trasher.

Finally, he was able to tear his eyes away from that awful act, unable to look at her any longer, face twisted in agony as if his features would stay frozen like that forever, caught in a storm of emotions he could not suppress or subdue. Flashes before his eyes now. Of Vaughn Masterson's exploding face when the bullet struck him. His grandfather's body twisting in the air as he fell.

He ran. Across the street, dodging the cars, knowing that cars would not hit him because he was on a mission. As he reached the other side of the street, he continued running, his mind filled with visions. Visions of what he would do to her. He pictured her sitting in a chair, all tied up—her arms and legs—but her chest free. He did not want to tie down her chest, although he wasn't sure why. He would not touch her after tying her down. He would play with her as if she were a toy. He would let something else touch her. Like a knife. He would let the knife do the touching like that old TV commercial, let your fingers do the walking. But the knife would do the walking, all over her body and her chest. She would be afraid. He would see in her eyes how she would be afraid. She deserved to be afraid. After what she had done with that trasher. She would be afraid of that knife and afraid of The Avenger.

After making her afraid, he would do to her what he had done to Vaughn Masterson and his grandfather.

First of all, of course, he would have to make his plans. Carefully and cleverly. Must draw her into his trap. Must strike at the right moment.

I am The Avenger, he cried silently, a cry of triumph that soared within him even as he stumbled along the street.

Eleven years old but smarter and wiser than ever before.

Jane had just turned into the corner of Arbor Drive when she encountered Amos Dalton waving to her from across the street.

She waved back distractedly, eager to get home and report Karen's progress to her parents. In the week since Karen emerged from the coma, she had struggled to speak but had not uttered words that could be understood. Suddenly this afternoon, she managed to say "Hello Jane" not clearly or distinctly and not without effort that bathed her face with perspiration. But saying the words clearly enough to be understood. *Hello Jane.* Wonderful. Buddy, too, would be impressed. He still had not met her. The doctor insisted that only family members visit her during this precarious time.

Amos Dalton had stopped waving and was running toward her now, crossing the street, running awkwardly with three books pressed to his chest.

"You've got to come with me, Jane," he said. "It's an emergency."

"What kind of an emergency?" she asked. Kids were always exaggerating and Amos Dalton, middle-aged kid in his laced-up shoes, was probably no exception.

"I can't tell you—you've got to see for yourself." His chin trembled, his lips were bluish. "It's a matter of life and death."

She hesitated, in a hurry to be on her way but wanting to do the right thing if it *was* an emergency.

"Please," he begged. As he shifted his position the books spilled to the sidewalk. "You've got to come." Not moving to pick up the books. Amos Dalton: book lover, not picking up his books. He must be desperate. Turning away, he took a few tentative steps, calling over his shoulder: "Come on . . ."

"Hey, how about your books?"

"The heck with them," he said, hurrying away. "Please come . . ."

"God, this must really be important," she muttered, picking up the books as she began to follow him. Two paperbacks, Stephen King kind of books with gruesome covers plus a copy of *The Adventures of Tom Sawyer*.

"Where are we going?" Jane called as Amos Dalton stretched the distance between them.

"Not far. But we've got to hurry."

At the corner of Arbor Lane and Vista Drive, Amos Dalton gave her another quick over-the-shoulder glance and plunged into the overgrown grass and shrubs of an empty lot. The tall grass almost hid a sign: LAND FOR SALE. She barely saw Amos Dalton's head above the wild growth.

Stopping at the edge of the lot, she called: "I'm not going in there unless you tell me what's going on. . . ."

Amos Dalton paused, his face barely visible above the thick undergrowth. "It's Artie." His voice cracked a bit. "Something's the matter with him." Desperate suddenly.

"Why didn't you say that in the first place?" she said, alarmed, remembering Artie's nighttime terrors. She threw aside all caution along with her fear of snakes which might be crawling around underfoot and followed him into the abandoned lot. The grass, damp from a recent rain, brushed moistly against her legs, a slimy feeling that made her shudder with distaste.

Amos Dalton thrashed his way ahead; she almost lost sight of him. She dropped one of the books and said, "The hell with it," walking unsteadily through the growth, like trying to walk in a foot of water. At length, the growth dwindled into a crooked path that led to an abandoned part of the neighborhood, woods where kids played their mysterious games. She saw a shed with sagging roof and boarded-up windows, set against a stand of pine trees. She had never explored this part of the neighborhood. This was a kids' kind of spot, just the sort of place Artie and his brat pack would choose for their fun and games.

"I hope this isn't a trick," she called to Amos, a bit of anger diluting her fear for Artie's safety.

"It's not a trick," Amos said, halting now and facing

her, perhaps ten feet away. Then pointing toward the shed:
"He's in there . . ."

She, too, stopped. The area was still. No birdcalls. No
barking dogs. No wind rustling in the trees. "Artie," she
called. "Are you okay?"

No answer. She took a few steps forward.

"In here," a voice reached her from the shed. A muffled voice, full of anguish, pain maybe. Could be Artie's
voice. "Hurry . . ." The word strangled, fading into a kind
of gasp.

She ran instinctively toward the shed, knowing that if
Artie was in trouble or some kind of danger, she simply
could not turn away or abandon him. In her peripheral
vision, she saw Amos Dalton scooting away, stumbling and
tripping in his haste to leave, raising her suspicions but not
compelling enough to make her change her course.

Out of breath, sweating now, aware of perspiration
moistening her body, she arrived at the door. "Artie," she
called. "Are you in there?"

The door swung open, revealing Mickey Looney, grinning at her, but a grin she had never seen before on his
face: cunning, triumphant, his eyes wide and gaping.

He held a rag in his hand. A peculiar smell emanated
either from Mickey or the rag or the hidden shadows of the
shed itself. He stepped toward her as she stepped backward, stumbled, almost fell. Mickey came closer, moving
more swiftly than she had ever seen him move, menacing,
grabbing her, the rag in her nostrils, the sweet, cloying
smell overwhelming her. She flailed about, trying to escape
Mickey's grasp and that sickening rag over her face. Just
before she slipped into blankness, as if sliding down a long
dark chute, she heard Mickey's gleeful voice saying:

"The Avenger strikes again."

* * *

She woke up suddenly, flashing into wakefulness, and found herself tied by clothesline rope to a chair, a foul-tasting rag stuffed in her mouth, her lips sealed with some kind of adhesive tape. Struggling to move, she realized she was helpless, wrists bound to the arms of a sturdy, throne-like chair, her ankles tied to its legs. The gag in her mouth threw her into a panic, threatening her with either suffocation or choking to death. Trying to calm herself, she squirmed to see how tightly she was secured. The rope chafed her wrists, dug into the flesh of her ankles. Breathing through her nostrils, she inhaled the smell of decay.

The sun slanting through a crack in the roof faintly illuminated the shed in which she was held captive. The shed was cluttered with debris, rusting tools, boxes stuffed with old rags, newspapers piled up in tottering stacks. She hated to look too closely at her surroundings, afraid to see rats scurrying around the floor or spiders crawling up the walls.

The door swung open and a slash of sunlight burst against her eyeballs. A dark bulk filled the doorway, blocking the sudden brightness. When the door closed, she saw Mickey Looney through the sunspots that danced in her eyes.

Instinctively, she tried to talk but emitted only strange animal-like sounds, the effort gagging her, making her retch. Afraid to choke, she fell silent.

As Mickey waddled toward her, she blinked with surprise, as if seeing him for the first time. He was fat but not really fat. Bloated, really. Bulging stomach, bulging cheeks. No eyebrows, which made his eyes unusually large, as if they'd pop out of their sockets if somebody squeezed his head. He was bareheaded—and bald. She had never seen him without that old baseball cap. He grinned at her, coming closer, bending over and peering down, curiously, as if she were a specimen in a laboratory or a strange animål in a zoo. The grin was not the old Mickey Looney grin but a leering evil grin, not the Mickey who mowed lawns and fed the birds.

Then the grin was gone and he was like the old Mickey Looney she knew, who patted kids on the head and tipped his cap to everybody.

"Are you all right, Jane?" His eyes studied her, roaming across her body. She tried to twist away from him but was helpless to move.

Once again, she tried to talk. Tried to say: Why are you doing this? But could only make weird sounds. And was still afraid of choking.

Still regarding her curiously, he said: "I can take that rag out of your mouth if you promise not to scream." She nodded vigorously. "Even if you scream, nobody will hear you and it will make The Avenger mad."

She remembered that he had mentioned The Avenger when he had slapped that terrible rag across her mouth and nose. Who was The Avenger?

Still nodding vigorously, she tried to make her eyes say what her mouth could not.

He tenderly pulled the adhesive bandage from her mouth, tugging at it gently. His gentleness encouraged her. Her mouth was finally free. She tried to spit out the taste of foulness. Her teeth ached.

"Why are you doing this, Mickey?" she sputtered at last. "What's the matter with you?"

"Nothing's the matter with me, Jane," he said, stepping backward, hands on his hips, eyes still popped open. "It's you. Something's the matter with you."

"What are you talking about?" Her voice rising, anger overcoming her fear of this crazy situation.

"Don't yell—don't scream. If you scream, I'll have to

do to you what I did to Vaughn Masterson and my grandfather." He put his hand to his mouth, and giggled. "Of course, I'm going to do that to you anyway but not right away. . . ."

She did not have to ask him what he had done to Vaughn Somebody-or-other or his grandfather. She could easily guess from the look on his face, the matter-of-fact way he spoke. More chilling than ghoulish laughter.

"Why, Mickey? Why?" she asked again. No other question mattered at the moment. If he answered that question, she would know the answer to all questions.

"Because you were with him," he said, petulant, a child suddenly.

"With who?"

"With your boyfriend."

"Buddy? Buddy Walker?"

"Is that his name? I don't know his name but you were with him. You were holding hands with him. And . . ." Now he frowned, a strand of spittle at the corner of his mouth. "You kissed him. You put your tongue in his mouth . . ." Spitting on the floor now, as if to rid himself of something vile and foul-tasting.

"You're angry with me because I have a boyfriend and kissed him?" she asked, astonished.

"No, no," he said, shaking his head. "You're pretty and you should have a boyfriend."

"Because I kissed him?" Trying to recall his exact words. "Because I touched his tongue with my tongue . . ."

"That wasn't nice," he said. "But if you wanted to do it, you could do it . . ."

"Then why are you so angry?"

"Because it's him!" Loud, shouting, stamping his foot, his jowls moving like Jell-O in a bowl.

Struggling against the ropes, ignoring the painful chafing her struggle caused, she raised her own voice. "I don't know what you're talking about." Her anger buoyed her, gave her hope and confidence. "What the hell are you talking about?"

"You shouldn't swear, Jane," he said. "Nice girls don't swear." Shaking his head sadly. "But you're not a nice girl anymore, are you? You were with him so you can't be nice . . ."

She sagged in the chair, as much as the ropes allowed. She could smell her own perspiration, her hair was damp, a lock fallen across one eye. She blew air out of the corner of her mouth.

Mickey reached out, pushed the lock of hair away.

"Him," he whispered, face close to hers now. The word imbued with all the hate one small syllable could convey. "Him, Jane. Your boyfriend. One of *them*. One of them in your house that night. I saw them, saw *him* wrecking your house. I was at the window and watched them. They didn't see me but I saw them, all right. And he was one of them."

Buddy? In her house?

"They were like animals," he said, drawing away, speaking quickly now, his eyes bulging even wider. "Breaking everything. Running through your house, screaming and laughing. Like animals."

Shaking her head, she heard herself saying: "No, no, no." Denying what this crazy person was saying.

"I saw Karen come in and they grabbed her." Then whispering: "The lights went out . . ."

A final gasping "No," a harrowing scream of a word torn from her throat in a spasm of denial.

"Yes, yes, yes, yes," he said, leaping in the air, dancing, his lumbering body shaking the floorboards. "And the other day you held his hand and I saw you. You looked at him like you loved him. In that video store, you put your lips on his lips and put your tongue in his mouth." The dance over, breathing heavily, standing before her, rivulets of sweat pouring down his cheeks. "That's why I have to do what I have to do, Jane. I am The Avenger and I must avenge your house. . . ."

The nausea engulfed her stomach so suddenly that she gasped in surprise as the vomit erupted from her mouth, burning her throat with acid, gushing through her lips in a sickening torrent. Her body responded painfully, her stomach stretched beyond its limits because she could not move, could not bend forward to ease the flow of vomit and for an eternal moment, the vomit blocked her throat and she coughed, choking, panic rushing through her, until it gushed forth again, spewing out of her mouth, spilling on her blouse, her skirt, splashing to the floor.

Mickey Looney leaped out of the way but flecks of vomit, pink and orange, splashed on his trousers and he cried out, "Oh, oh," again and again, "Oh, oh." Then stood fascinated, watching her retch.

Wrists and ankles stinging with rope burns, stomach heaving, the taste of foulness in her mouth, the smell of her own vomit filling her nostrils, Jane sank into an abysmal despair that made the nausea and the stench of vomit pale by comparison. Buddy a trasher? One of them? Her Buddy? Whom she'd love with a love that was bigger than her own life. Buddy who had kissed her and caressed her, held her breasts so tenderly.

Mickey was dancing around again, a dance of desperation now. "I'm sorry, I'm sorry," he said. He found another rag and began to wipe her face, her chin, dabbing at her chest, his hand lingering on her breast.

"Now can you see what I have to do?" he said, leaping away from her, his face flushed, avoiding her eyes.

She did not ask what he had to do, still stunned by what he had said about Buddy, trying to deny the truth of his accusation. Mickey gazed at her breasts and looked away again. Would he rape her?

"I have to remove you from the world, Jane."

The thought of Buddy fled as she realized what he was saying. "You mean—kill me?" she said, aghast, the terrible words blazing in the air. She was immediately sorry that she had said the words, as if speaking them made them real.

"That's the only way, Jane. I have to do it . . ."

Her mind raced, seeking arguments, *anything* to stave him off. "Why me, Mickey?" Needing to stall, play for time. Had to use everything at her disposal. Including Buddy, guilty or not. "Why not my boyfriend? He was one of the trashers you said. I didn't trash my house—he did." Felt like a traitor to Buddy now, even if he *did* trash her house. Yet, a small part of her denying that Mickey would actually kill her or Buddy.

"Oh, I'm going to do it to him, too," he said. "To all of them. The Avenger must seek his revenge. I am eleven years old and must avenge your house."

Had she heard correctly? Had she missed a beat?

"What did you say?"

Speaking distinctly, emphasizing every syllable, he said: "I am eleven years old and I am The Avenger and must avenge your house. . . ."

"But you're not eleven years old. You're Mickey Stallings and you're not The Avenger." Whoever The Avenger was. Some comic-book hero he was confused about?

"Oh, I'm eleven all right," he said, smiling, docile

childlike now. "Whenever I'm on the job as The Avenger, I'm always eleven years old."

Keep him talking, and don't think about Buddy.

"Why are you eleven, Mickey?" she asked, wanting to spit the residue of foulness out of her mouth but forcing herself to swallow. "What happened to you that makes you eleven again?" Shots in the dark, shooting out words without knowing the target of those words.

"Vaughn Masterson," he declared, triumph in his voice. "That was my best time. The best time of my life. Know what it feels like to remove someone like Vaughn Masterson from the world, Jane? A bully who was mean to other kids? It was beautiful, Jane. But then my gramps got suspicious of me. He began to ask me questions and I became eleven again so that I could remove *him* from the world. Became eleven like with Vaughn Masterson." He smiled at her, pride in the smile, as if he had revealed to her the pride of his life, the sum of his accomplishments. "Poor Mickey Stallings had to grow up and get big and his mother died and he remembers all the things his mother told him and the songs she sang. But Mickey Stallings can still be eleven." He raised his eyes to the sagging wooden ceiling. "Eleven and The Avenger." He looked down at her and Mickey Stallings was gone. The old Mickey who had repaired broken faucets and planted tomatoes and who tipped his hat to everyone.

From somewhere in the folds of his flesh around his waist, he drew a knife. A kitchen knife but a big one. The kind turkeys are sliced with. A blade that gleamed even in the dimness of this godforsaken shed.

Stall, she commanded herself. She was dealing with a madman and had to stall him off. She also knew she had nothing to lose. Her world had already ended, in a way. With the knowledge that Buddy had trashed her house. All doubts gone. He had sought her out and trashed her. With his kisses and his caresses. She saw clearly now why he had avoided her house and the hospital. Why he drank. Buddy, Buddy, she thought, and he was part of the stench of vomit that surrounded her, part of Mickey Looney and what he was doing to her, what he planned to do to her. But stall. Forget everything else, forget Buddy and Karen and every thing else. She had to survive, get away, escape.

"The only person I ever loved was my mother," Mickey said, holding the knife in both hands as if it was an offering to Jane. "I loved my mother but I liked you Jane."

Chilled at the past tense of *like,* she said: "I always liked you, too, Mickey. You were always kind and gentle to everyone." Noticing her own use of the past tense, which seemed more chilling than his.

"I used to watch you undress in your room. Until you started pulling down the shades. That made me sad . . ."

"I'm sorry it made you sad," she said, shivering with the knowledge he had watched her taking off her clothes.

Although he still held the knife balanced in the palm of his hands, he had become gentle again, his voice normal like the Mickey she had known.

Think, she urged herself. Outthink him.

"How about Amos Dalton?" she asked.

"What about him?" Suspicious, eyes narrowing.

"He looked scared when he led me here. How did you get him to do that?" Keep him talking.

"He likes books. I gave him ten dollars to buy books." Brightening, eyes popping again.

"I don't think he's out buying books," she said. "I think he might be calling the police."

Mickey shook his head. "He won't call the police. I gave him ten dollars. . . ."

She was surprised at how sharp and clear her mind was, rising above the stench that surrounded her, that came from her. Shaking her head, she said: "He told me to be careful in here. I think he was suspicious, Mickey. He said if I didn't come out in ten minutes, he was going to call the cops. . . ."

Mickey tilted his head, appraising her differently now, not like a denizen of a zoo.

Mickey smiled, a wide smile that revealed his teeth. "You think The Avenger isn't smart," he said. "You think you can fool him . . ."

"I'm not trying to fool you. I'm only telling you what Amos Dalton said."

Mickey took the knife in his right hand, brandishing it, slashing at the air with the long blade. "Well, if the cops are on the way, then The Avenger has to work fast." He giggled, coming closer. "Won't he? It's better to work fast, anyway. That way it won't hurt you so much."

He stood looking at her, face still with sadness, eyes full of regret. In that instant, she knew that he was really going to kill her. If he had continued to rant and rave, jump up and down, giggle or scream, she would have held out hope for herself.

Give me time to say a prayer. That was what she was about to say. One last request, beyond panic now, accepting the situation. "No," she cried out, denying her panic, her acceptance. It wasn't supposed to happen this way. *I am sixteen years old and I am not going to die this way.* This was Mickey Stallings in front of her. Not The Avenger, not some monstrous eleven-year-old. She had to make him see who he really was.

"Know how old you are, Mickey?" she asked, trying to keep the desperation out of her voice.

"I am not Mickey. I am The Avenger."

"You can't be The Avenger. The Avenger is eleven years old."

"I *am* eleven," he said, the knife dangling from his hand, his voice petulant.

"No, you're not."

"Yes, I am."

Like children arguing in the schoolyard.

"Know why you're not eleven?"

Curious, he tilted his head. "Why?"

"Because if you were really eleven years old, you wouldn't be looking at me all the time. At my blouse, my breasts." As if hypnotized by her words, he looked at her chest. Remembering how he had touched her breast with the rag in his hand, she said, "Eleven-year-old boys don' do that. But you do. You're doing it now. You're looking at my chest now."

He took his eyes away. She saw the guilt in those big eyes.

"Did you touch me when you tied me up? Feel my chest? Eleven-year-old boys don't do that, either. If you did that, then you're not The Avenger, not eleven . . ."

"I am The Avenger," he said, appalled, eyes bulging again. "I'm The Avenger and I avenge the bad things in the world and I'm eleven years old."

"You were eleven a long time ago, Mickey. When you killed that bully. That was bad. But you are not eleven anymore. And I'm not a bully. I'm Jane Jerome and you're Mickey Stallings. . . ."

"I'm . . . ." He was at a loss now for words, frowning his mouth open, pink tongue fluttering against his lips, his eyes flickering to her chest and away.

"*You* killed your grandfather," she said. "The Avenger didn't do it. You did. Mickey Stallings. What would you mother say if she knew? Your mother would be mad at you, would punish you."

"No," he cried. "No."

"Yes." Straining against the ropes that held her, cheeks stiff with caked vomit, hair falling across her eyes, wrists chafed, eyes searing. "Yes, yes, yes." Each syllable erupting out of her fear and her determination and her desperation. "You killed your grandfather . . . your grandfather who loved you."

"No," he cried again. Anguished, the word like a howling in the air . . . nooooooooooo . . . drawn out . . . noooooooo . . . echoing in the dusty shed . . . terror and tears in the word. . . . nooooooo . . . and pain and futility . . . noooooooo . . .

He sank down on the floor, looked at the knife as if seeing it for the first time. He lifted his hand, and turned his wrist and slashed it with the knife. "I loved my Gramps," he said. "He took me to the movies and bought me M&Ms and then we grabbed some grub." He looked at the blood oozing out of his wrist. "The Avenger made me do it." Looking at Jane, huge tears in the huge eyes. "I didn't want to do it." Then looking back at his wrist, the blood dripping now, onto the floor. He switched the knife into his other hand, the action slow and deliberate, watching his hand doing it, and Jane, astonished, felt that she was seeing two people before her, poor old gentle and kindly Mickey Stallings and the eleven-year-old Avenger who was killing him. Now he slashed the other wrist and watched calmly, curiously, as the blood gushed forth, the incision deeper than the first cut, the blood spurting in the air as if from a miniature fountain in his flesh. He took the knife and plunged it into his stomach, groaning and turning to look at her. "Mommy," he said, looking up at Jane. "Mommy . . ." Voice fading, blood spreading now across his shirt, the smell of blood—did blood actually have a smell?—mingling with the smell of vomit in her nostrils.

Watching his life ebbing away, she felt part of herself ebbing away, too, as her thoughts returned to Buddy. Buddy, her betrayer.

"Jane," Mickey murmured, raising his head, trying to say more, mouth moving, a pleading in his eyes, tiny bubbles forming on his lips, uttering sounds she could not recognize, dying sounds. Poor Mickey Looney.

As he closed his eyes the door swung open and two police officers were suddenly stomping into the shed while sirens howled outside. Dazed by the sudden activity, she saw Amos Dalton, still clutching his books, standing in the doorway in his laced-up, middle-aged shoes. "Sorry it took so long," he said, and burst into tears.

Poor all of us, Jane thought, as her own tears finally came.

Buddy did not learn of Jane's ordeal until eleven o'clock that night. He and Jane had not planned to see each other that evening: she and her mother were off on a shopping spree at the Mall for summer clothes. Buddy had decided to stay home and catch up on homework even though it was a Friday night. The house was eerily quiet. His mother had finally chosen that weekend to go off on her retreat after a lot of table talk, which was a relief from the usual dinnertime conversations. "If I go, will I be giving up control over my life?" That was her big question. "No worse than going to a therapist" was Addy's usual answer, which Buddy supported. Despite pangs of conscience Addy was spending the night at a friend's house, going over last-minute production problems with her school play. As she was about to leave she paused at the door, a look of concern on her face. "I'll be fine by myself—I'm not going to drink," he said. "I wasn't thinking about that," she said. "I just didn't want you to be lonesome." He nodded, didn't know what to say, touched by her concern.

He pondered going to the Mall and surprising Jane and her mother, probably buy them coffee at Friendly's. But he still did not feel comfortable with either of Jane's parents and decided to stay home. Did most of the homework. Heated a casserole of scalloped potatoes and ham slices that his mother had prepared beforehand. Fell asleep on the couch reading *Time* magazine. Woke up at ten-twenty astonished that he had slept that long.

He went to his bedroom, removed the bottle of gin from his hiding place in the closet, looked at it, thanked God for the presence of Jane Jerome in his life, and put it back. Someday he would really have to thank God but did not know exactly how. He conducted this ritual with the bottle every night, usually before he went to bed.

Downstairs again, bored, restless, he checked his watch. A bit before eleven. He turned on the television set, stared dully at the final scenes of a stupid comedy, the laugh track annoyingly loud. He had read somewhere that laugh tracks were recordings of audiences long ago, that most of the laughing people were probably dead by now.

Half dozing, he barely reacted to the newscaster who announced that among tonight's headlines was the abduction of a Burnside girl by a man who later committed suicide. Had the newscaster actually said Burnside? Burnside seldom figured in nightly newscasts on the Wickburg channel except for city council meetings and other dull stuff.

A moment later, his attention was drilled on the TV as the announcer said: "Drama in Burnside today as sixteen-year-old Jane Jerome escaped capture and possible death at the hands of her abductor, who committed suicide moments before her rescue." Flashes of a shed, woods, police milling about.

"Her abductor, forty-one-year-old Michael Stallings, stabbed himself several times and died as police broke into the shed, led by ten-year-old Amos Dalton, who had reported the abduction to them. The Jerome girl had been bound hand and foot to a chair in the shed. After a checkup at Burnside Hospital, she was reported unharmed."

Shots now of Arbor Lane, Jane's house, other houses, twilight shots, stark in floodlights, almost colorless, and then a swift glimpse of Jane, huddled between her parents and police, being hurried up the front steps.

"The Jerome family is now in seclusion elsewhere at this hour and their whereabouts are unknown. The family of young Amos Dalton has not allowed the boy to speak to the news media." Shot of a different house, the boy's evidently. "Police Chief Darrell Teague said that the investigation is continuing."

Buddy watched the images on the screen and listened to the voices without moving, although aware of the thudding of his heart. He thought: Did I really wake up a few minutes ago or am I still dreaming? He shook his head, to rouse himself, and the room went out of focus. His hand reached out to prevent him from plunging off the sofa in a swirl of dizziness. He remembered something from a long-ago first-aid lesson. Put your head between your legs to keep yourself from fainting. But he still did not move.

The telephone rang.

Like an alarm clock waking him up.

Suddenly, the details on the television screen achieved a stark reality—Jane had been kidnapped and then rescued—and he reached for the phone, knowing that she was calling him to tell him that she was fine, not to worry, everything was all right.

But Jane was not on the phone.

"I just saw on TV what happened to Jane," Addy said. "Are you okay?"

"Sure," he said. But was he okay? "I just saw it, too. On television . . ."

"You mean you didn't know about it?" Addy asked. "She didn't call? I mean, this happened, like, hours ago . . ."

He shook his head as if to deny Addy's remarks, groped for a response. "Everything looked so hectic," he said. "The announcer said she's in seclusion with her family. She'll call, Addy. When she gets a chance . . ."

"Of course, she will. Poor kid . . . this must be like a nightmare for her," Addy said. "Do you want me to come home, Buddy?"

"No, no," he said. "I'm fine. I know she'll call as soon as she can. I'd better hang up. She's probably trying to reach me right this minute. . . ."

He hung up. Then looked down at the phone, actually expecting it to ring. Waited. The house silent. *I need a drink.* But couldn't drink now. Had to keep sharp and alert in case she called and needed him at her side: *Please hurry, Buddy, please come . . .*

He glanced at the clock on the mantel. Twenty past eleven. Getting late. She should have called. Why hadn't she?

He picked up the phone, punched her number. He didn't count the rings, merely listened, long lonely sounds. No answer. Maybe he had touched the wrong number. Tried again, knowing it was useless, the words of the newscaster echoed in his mind: *The Jerome family is now in seclusion elsewhere.* Where was elsewhere?

Torn with the need to take some kind of action, he considered driving to her street. Perhaps she had left a message with neighbors. He cursed himself now for not making friends with her friends, her neighbors. He was a stranger to them. Anyway, why should she leave a message with neighbors when she could have called him? Or sent someone with a message? He had been home the entire evening. Slept awhile, yes, but the ringing of the phone or the doorbell would have awakened him.

Why hadn't she called?

He did not try to answer that question.

He awoke with a start, grubby in his clothes, which he had not removed before falling to sleep finally about four o'clock in the morning. He had dozed fitfully during the long hours of the night. Tossing and turning on the couch which allowed no room for tossing and turning, he had decided at three-thirty or so that she was never going to call. What would he do if she didn't? The solution came to him in a flash out of his desperation. And this decision allowed him finally to drift into a deep sleep but not deep enough or long enough.

Awake, the sun streaming in, he sat up on the couch. Stale taste in his mouth, head aching a bit, he remembered that he had not taken a drink, the only good thing about a bad night.

He reached for the phone, the movement automatic, punched her number. He did not expect an answer and did not get one. The clock said eight-ten. Time for the only action he could take, the plan he had devised during the night.

Twenty minutes later, he took up his vigil in the parking lot in the space that was nearest to the front entrance of the hospital. Weary, despondent, he watched the entrance. Tried not to blink. Tried not to think. Blink, think. Felt clever for thinking of the hospital, how sooner or later someone in Jane's family was certain to visit Karen. They would not abandon her despite what had happened to Jane. Slouching in his seat behind the wheel, he prepared himself for a long wait, a long day. Why hadn't she called? Let's not think about that. Don't blink and don't think. She has her reasons. But what reasons? What if . . . don't answer that question. No blinking and no thinking.

For an hour or so, he watched visitors come and go, heard a siren as an ambulance pulled up to the emergency entrance. Jane had told him that Karen's room was on the fourth floor front, third window from the right, and he watched the window for signs of movement, someone pulling the curtain aside, thinking that perhaps a visitor to Karen had somehow eluded him. No movement. He yawned, bored. Wished he had brought something to eat, wondered if there was a vending machine in the hospital lobby. Then decided he had better not leave the car or his vigil.

He woke up with a start, a horn blowing somewhere, and struck his chest on the steering wheel, eyes dazzled by the sun flashing on the windshield, limbs aching. Cripes, he had fallen asleep, couldn't believe it. Checked his watch—eleven-thirty. The parking lot had filled up. He looked up at Karen's room. The curtain was undisturbed.

A sudden rap on the window next to him made him jump, this time striking his elbow on the shift stick. He turned to find himself confronting the beefy face of a police officer, who motioned him to open the window. Buddy fumbled for the key. The windows were automatic, would not go up or down unless the motor was on. Turning the key, he listened to the engine leap with life and then hit the window button.

"Hello, Officer," Buddy said, still half asleep, trying to speak brightly, alertly.

"You been here quite a while, fella," the officer said. The badge on his chest read SECURITY #15.

"I've been waiting for someone." Speaking lamely, face flushed with guilt as if he were a criminal, for crissakes.

"Who might that be?" the officer asked, a hard edge to his voice.

"My mother," he said. "She said she'd meet me here but I think I missed her. I fell asleep . . ." Easy to lie when you are desperate.

The police officer obviously did not believe him, seemed to be pondering his next step. Then his face softened: "Look, kid, I don't know what this is all about but you'd better move on, okay?"

He drove out of the parking lot, roamed aimlessly for a while and then headed for Arbor Lane, where he cruised slowly down the street. Quick glances at Jane's house. Shades down, no signs of life. No car in the driveway. An empty house sends a lonely message: nobody home.

I'd better get home, maybe right this minute she's trying to reach me, he thought. Angry at himself for spending all that useless time at the hospital, he gunned the motor in a fury. The phone could be ringing right this minute at his house, echoing through the empty rooms.

At home, the house gathered him into its silence.

Why doesn't she call?

Why *hadn't* she called?

The beginning of an answer like a quivering worm crept into his mind.

He could no longer deny himself a drink and made his way upstairs to his bedroom where the bottle waited.

*   *   *

Blood suffused Jane's dreams during the two nights she and her family spent at the Monument Motel. Blood dripped from trees, gushed from springs, streamed from faucets, flowed through streets. Blood everywhere, on everything, swirling across the floor, seeping between her toes when she realized, to her horror, that she was barefoot. She could not run, the blood having turned to a crimson clinging ooze through which she waded helplessly.

She woke up, trembling in the unfamiliar room. Searched for signs of identity. Her body was sticky with perspiration which she feared was blood. She sat up on the edge of the bed, fumbled for the switch to the lamp, pressed it, the room blindingly bright, stinging her eyes. No blood on her body, her pajamas limp only with dampness. Artie slept in the twin bed next to hers. Her father and mother slept in the adjoining room, the door between left open. She sat there miserably, her feet touching the carpet, shivering slightly yet savoring these moments alone. She had not been alone since her departure from the cabin, the last signs of life pulsing out of Mickey Looney. A frenzy of activity, police, ambulance, television cameras, reporters, all of it a mad swirl. Her father became her protector, her salvation and strength. Even the police abided by his rules as he limited questions at police headquarters, his arm around her shoulder in the cruiser on the way home. Her street was hectic with people, cars, bicycles, faces she did not recognize, everyone trying to peek at her as if she were some rare specimen brought home from Mars by explorers.

Her father decreed no interviews with the news media and kept his word despite the battering questions, the angry reactions of reporters and newscasters clustered on the sidewalk in front of her house. Peering out once, she recognized a newscaster from the Wickburg TV station. Noth-

ing, however, impinged on her. She was numb inside, even
her thought processes in limbo.

Everyone seemed to be whispering and in the whispers
she heard words like *courageous* and *heroic* but did not feel
courageous or heroic. Chief Reardon from Monument, her
father's old golfing buddy, arrived along with her favorite
relatives, her aunt Josie and uncle Rod. Her family rallying
around. She heard her mother say: *this place,* anger in her
voice. We'll be moving, she thought, but the words were
meaningless. She had not had time to think, while being
driven to the hospital for a checkup, then to the police
station, answering the questions, signing reports, coming
home, into her mother's arms. "Better rest, lie down
awhile," her mother had said. But she did not want to rest,
did not want to lie down even for a while, did not want to
be alone. Because once she was alone she would begin to
think. And she would think of Buddy. Everyone thought
she was stricken with the events of her ordeal, everyone
thought she was stunned and shocked because of poor
Mickey Looney. But it was Buddy all the time. Buddy who
had betrayed her. Buddy who had trashed her house and
later trashed her, desecrated her. She had loved him, built
her world around him and their future together.

They were like prisoners in the house, the crowds lingering outside. Chief Reardon came up with the solution.
"Let's get her away from here for a couple of days till the
heat dies down." He talked like an old movie tough guy.
"Come on back to Monument, the wife and I'll put you
up." In the end, they drove away, back to Monument, elud-
ing reporters' cars. At the motel, she swallowed the pill Dr.
Allison had given her. Sleep came in a wave of blood.

Now she sat on the edge of the bed, listening to the
sleep sounds of Artie, the familiar snoring of her father
from the next room. She was finally, truly alone. With her

thoughts. Her thoughts of Buddy. She had not mentioned
to anyone what Mickey Looney had revealed about Buddy,
pretended innocence about Mickey's motives for abducting
her. No one pressed her or seemed suspicious, took it for
granted that Mickey had simply picked her at random.
Buddy's part in the nightmare was her secret, which she
would never divulge to anyone.

At one point before leaving the house in Burnside, her
mother said: "What about Buddy?"

She shook her head. Did not trust herself to speak.
Then spoke anyway. "I'll call him later," she said, turning
away from her mother's puzzled expression. Her mother
said no more, kept her suspicions, if she had any, to herself.

Alone now at three o'clock in the morning, she
thought of what F. Scott Fitzgerald had written—*In a real
dark night of the soul it is always three o'clock in the morning.* Spoken by her teacher in the classroom, those words
had left her unmoved, probably because she had seldom
been awake at three o'clock in the morning. Now she knew
the desolation of the words and how it felt to be so alone,
abandoned, and betrayed. Oh, Buddy, she thought. You've
done this to us. Everything could have been so wonderful.

She climbed back into bed, reached for the light
switch, and was grateful for the darkness. She thought of
Buddy at home, waiting for her call, wondering why she
hadn't called. She took consolation, imagining his misery.
Let him be miserable, too. She clung to the thought although tears formed in her eyes. Damn him, damn him.
Why did he have to spoil everything? But realized that he
had already spoiled everything even before they met and
fell in love, hadn't he? Had trashed their love before it had
even happened.

Sleep, dark and ugly, came at last as the first fingernails of dawn pried at the motel room's draperies.

"Buddy?"

Her voice saying his name trembled in his ear and he pressed the receiver closer, afraid that he might miss every nuance and tone.

"Yes," he said. Then, needlessly: "Jane?" Because he knew it was Jane, of course, would know that voice anywhere. And without waiting for an answer said: "Are you okay?" Relief sweeping the words out of him: "Jane, I was so worried. I didn't know what to think." Unable to stop talking, "Where are you? I've been trying to reach you. Your phone doesn't answer. . . . I drove by your house a thousand times. . . ." *Why don't you please shut up and let her speak?*

"I'm okay," she said, almost a whisper, the ghost of a voice. "I'm home. Can you come over?"

"Of course. Sure, anytime. When?" *Stupid, stop talking* but soaring inside. She had called. The long agony ended. But a warning bell going off inside him. Her voice so subdued. Yes, but she's been through such an ordeal. She wouldn't be telling jokes, making wisecracks. He wanted to ask her a thousand questions.

"Right now. Can you come over right now?" she asked.

"I'll be there before you know it," he said, but lingering on the phone a minute.

"Okay," she said and hung up. Gone. Her voice a still soft echo in his mind.

As soon as he saw her face, he knew that it was over. That she had found out about him and did not love him anymore. He saw the knowledge in her eyes, flat and wounded, in her features as if set in stone, a hard flint face. He would never have thought it possible for her to look at him like this. Distant and cold, as if looking at him from a great distance, even though she stood only a few feet in front of him.

She knows, he thought. About me and this house.

"Come in," she said, stepping back.

"What's the matter?" he asked. "Are you okay?" His words hollow and meaningless, going-through-the-motions words. What killed him was this: She was so beautiful even in her coldness.

"Come in, Buddy," she said. "I want you to come in." Her voice giving orders.

Obeying the command, he stepped inside, dreading the moment he would enter this hallway where her sister had been pinned against the wall. He kept his eyes fastened on Jane's eyes, did not want to see the cellar door through which her sister had plunged. Did not want to look toward the stairway where he had stood with a bottle of vodka. Did not want to *think* about her room upstairs.

"I know why you never wanted to come into this house," she said. "My house."

Buddy said nothing, could say nothing, the mechanisms of his body not working.

"Because of what you did here."

And now the impact of her knowledge struck him, like a giant mallet hitting a gong inside him, the vibrations echoing throughout his body. For one impossible moment, he went blind, blacked out, and then came back again, her face and eyes piercing him.

"I didn't mean . . ." he began, then stopped, realizing that he could never explain to her what had happened, or why it had happened. He could not explain, even to himself.

"You trashed my house," she said. "Did you trash my bedroom, too? Tear my bed apart? Vomit on the carpet? Piss on the wall?"

The word *piss* shocked him. She never swore. That one word, *piss,* spelled his doom. He knew that as soon as she said it. He was linked in her mind with pissing.

"To think I loved you," she said. And now there was sadness in her voice and in this sadness hope renewed itself in him. Maybe there was a chance. "To think that I let you kiss me and touch me. And I kissed you back." Her arms had been hanging loose at her sides but now she wrapped them around her chest.

"Jane . . ." he said. But could say no more. He had heard of people being speechless and knew now exactly what that meant. He wanted to say so much, defend himself even when there was no defense, but could not speak, could not find the words and even if he could find them did not know how he would express them, where to begin even.

"You make me sick," she said, shivering, as if the fury of her words alone truly sickened her. "I don't want you here in this house, don't want you in my life. I only wanted you to come in here one more time. Now, get out. Out of my house. Out of my life . . ."

Did her voice break on that final word?

He didn't know. All he knew was that he said *Jane* and wasn't sure later whether he had said it out loud or tried to speak. Could not remember afterward. Remembered only the pale fury of her face, her eyes blazing not like fire but like ice, remembered standing there mute, absolutely numbed, and then turning, almost running into the door which was still open, turning away from her whom he loved with such desperation and desire, and running, running down the walk, running to the car, knowing that he was guilty of what she had said, knowing that he was one of the bad guys, after all.

She had just returned from visiting Karen in the hospital when Harry Flowers called.

Her visits to Karen were the only moments of light and gladness—not gladness exactly but absence of sadness, perhaps—in the grayness that her life had become. Able to speak again, Karen was a nonstop talker, filled with plans for resuming her life, shopping for new clothes, seeing all her friends. Her hospital room was filled with gifts from her classmates, crazy get-well cards on the bulletin board, balloons floating above her bed, flowers everywhere. Although Karen delighted in all the attention, a shadow sometimes crossed her features. She still could not remember what had happened on the night of the trashing. Her memory was a blank beyond the point where she opened the door and stepped into the house. For which Jane was grateful.

Jane was also grateful that her abduction and subsequent escape had disappeared quickly from the newspapers and television. The fact that Mickey Stallings left no survivors and his earlier crimes happened thirty years ago in a small town in Maine five hundred miles away contributed to the swift neglect of the story. The media lost interest in Jane and Amos Dalton when interviews were refused and Amos was packed away to relatives in Indiana. Poor Amos, who had done the brave thing in the end. Someday, when he returned, she would tell him how courageous he had been, after all.

No one in the family spoke of the future, whether they would remain in Burnside or move away. Jane was certain they would stay. One afternoon, she went by Artie's room and heard again the weird blips and bleeps from his video game and found herself smiling. Artie himself brought up the subject at the dinner table that night. "Are we going to move, Dad?" he asked, frowning, making one of his grotesque bratty faces. "We'll make a decision later," her father said. "When Karen is back from the hospital." Glancing tenderly at Jane: "And Jane has sorted out her feelings . . ."

Jane had no feelings to sort out. That was the problem. Her ordeal with Mickey had taken on an aspect of unreality, as if it had happened in a dream long ago. She had refused efforts to have her consult a psychiatrist. She did not have nightmares. The episode had been so brief, so fast-moving, that she could not remember all the details. She pitied Mickey Looney, would never forget his pain and anguish as she sat helplessly bound to the chair. She was not convinced that he would have actually killed her. She was surprised at her ability to relegate Mickey and the events in that shed to a distant corner of her mind.

Buddy was different. For the first few days, he was a pain in her heart. Knew that sounded dramatic but she actually felt that her heart was fiery with pain, like a knife blade twisting and turning in it. She knew vaguely that she still loved him. But also knew it was an impossible love. The damage was too great—the damage to her house, her life, her heart. If he had confessed earlier . . . if he had told her what he did and explained why . . . she might have felt differently. But she would never know. The worst thing is that she could not talk to anyone about Buddy. Merely told her family that the relationship was over.

"Did something happen in that shed to affect how you feel about him?" her mother asked, and Jane looked up sharply, amazed at her mother's astuteness.

"No," she said, conscious of lying but finding no other

way to answer. "We were beginning to drift apart anyway . . ."

Doubtful glances from her mother in the next few hours did not change Jane's decision to remain with the lie.

Often at night, before sleep came, his image formed itself in her mind. She would think of him in this room, on a rampage, the pee stains on the wall. She imagined the stains still there under the paint. Is that what he had become: pee stains on the wall? She sometimes cried just before falling off to sleep. Strange crying, without tears.

One morning, she opened her eyes and saw only the bare walls without posters or pictures. Something was different. But what? The sun edged into the room along the borders of the window shades. She threw off the blankets and sat up, glanced as always at that certain spot on the wall, trying to see under the paint. *She* was different. Not the room. The ache of Buddy's loss was absent. No pain at all, no anger. No odor under the surface, either. Just this hole inside of her now, like that black hole in space, and all her emotions, anger, regret, sorrow, had been pulled into that hole. She slipped out of bed, raised the shades, closing her eyes against the invasion of the sun. Then drew back, testing herself. How she felt. She felt—nothing. Numb. Vacant. Half believed that if she cut herself at this instant, no blood would flow from her veins. As if her veins were as empty as her body. Buddy was really gone now, not only from her life and her days and nights, but from herself or whatever she was deep inside. Had it really been love, then, if it could abandon her like this? What would take its place? Could you go through your life without feeling anything? She had read somewhere that nature hated a vacuum. This vacuum inside her now—what would move into it?

Harry Flowers called that day.

A pleasant aroma filled the house as she picked up the phone: her mother was boiling carrots spiced with cinnamon in the kitchen.

"Hello, Jane Jerome?"

"Yes," she said, hesitant. She did not recognize the caller's voice.

"Listen, you don't know me. But you know my name. My name is Harry Flowers." Then quickly, at her intake of breath: "Wait, don't hang up, please don't do anything. Just listen, that's all, a minute, two minutes. Just let me say what I have to say . . ."

Her mother came to the door, peered in questioningly. Jane shook her head, gave her an it's-not-important look and her mother returned to the kitchen.

"What I have to say is this: You've got Buddy Walker all wrong. Sure, he was with me and the others that night at your house. But he was drunk, didn't really know what he was doing. He didn't touch your sister. What happened to your sister was an accident whether you believe it or not, but Buddy had no part in it . . ."

"Why are you telling me this?" she asked, surprised at how calm and reasonable she sounded. How cool.

"I owe him this call. Look, I don't even like him. He's the kind of guy that I can't stand. Thinks he's better than other people, including yours truly. But he's sorry about what he did that night. His father and mother were getting divorced and I took advantage of his crappy life. That's why he got drunk and came with us to your house."

I should hang up, she thought. But didn't. She was curious. She wondered what Harry Flowers looked like. Wondered if she had already seen him on the street or at the Mall without realizing it. She tried to imagine his face, his features. But saw only Buddy in her mind.

"Buddy's in trouble. He's drinking again. He stopped for a while but now he's drinking more than ever."

She heard him take a deep breath.

"I was thinking," he said, his voice becoming intimate, like a caress in her ear. "Maybe we could get together sometime." Smooth, sly. "You know, to talk about all this. Just you and me . . ."

The telephone was suddenly like a snake in her hand. She dropped it to the floor and let it lie there for a moment before slamming it down on the receiver.

Jane and Buddy met by accident at the Mall on a Saturday afternoon in November, five months later.

She had been purposely avoiding the Mall, shopping instead at the small specialty stores on Main Street in Wickburg or a new shopping center that had opened a few miles away, near Monument.

He haunted the Mall, hoping to see her. Went out of his way to roam the stores, lurking near the entrances, sitting on the edge of the plastic bench in the lobby. The fountain still was not working, peeling even more than ever these days.

He sometimes drove to Burnside High in the afternoon and parked near the entrance—but not too near—hoping to catch glimpses of her. The sight of her walking along, her book bag slung over her shoulder, caused him such anguish and longing that tears sprang to his eyes and his chest hurt. He vowed not to return but always did.

On that November afternoon, they met face-to-face as he stepped off the down escalator and she approached the up.

Caught by surprise, she frowned, annoyed at herself for agreeing to meet her mother at Filene's, having forgotten her intention to avoid places where she might run into him.

"Hello, Jane," he said.

Although the Pizza Palace was several doors away, the smell of tomato sauce and pepperoni spiced the air with reminders.

He was pale. He had lost weight. She had once thought his blue eyes were beautiful. Now they were more gray than blue. The whites of his eyes laced with red.

"How have you been?" he asked.

She had wondered how she would react when they met again. "Good," she said. She had no reaction. He might have been a stranger. Not to be needlessly cruel, she asked: "How are you?"

Her question energized him, the fact that she had inquired about him. "Fine," he said. "I'm doing real good in school this year. All A's and B's so far." Had to keep talking, had to keep her here. Silence would take her away. "Things are fine at home. I mean, my mother and father are definitely getting divorced but it's a friendly divorce. Addy is doing fine, and my mother's doing fine, too."

How many times have I said fine? "I don't drink anymore. I'm concentrating on my studies . . ."

"Good," she said. He was obviously lying. She was amazed that he had once been able to deceive her so easily.

He realized that she had said *good* twice but had made no other comment except for that one question. He wanted to ask about her sister, Karen, but couldn't do that because it would bring up the subject of what had happened at her house. His mind skittered, went askew—how many times he had dreamed of meeting her like this, arranging conversations in his mind, what he would say and what she would say, and was now speechless. More than that: without thought, the way it happened sometimes in class when he gave an oral talk and everything went blank.

"Well, I have to go," she said. "My mother's waiting for me—I'm already late."

"Jane," he said, unable to let her go.

She paused, half-turned toward him, not saying anything, waiting.

His mind cleared and he found himself speaking words he had rehearsed countless times in his head, words to make her remember the good times.

"It was beautiful there for a while, wasn't it, Jane?"

He looked as if he were about to cry.

She thought of the trashing and Karen in the coma all that time and Mickey Looney dead and her father and mother and Artie. And those yellow stains under the paint in her bedroom.

"Was it?" she said, suddenly sorry for him, so sorry. As pity moved into that hole inside her, she discovered how distant pity was from hate, how very far it was from love.

She stepped on the escalator and slowly ascended, not looking back, leaving him down below.

A NEW PSYCHOLOGICAL THRILLER FROM
ROBERT CORMIER

0-385-32590-8

Francis Joseph Cassavant is 18. He has just returned home from World War II, and he has no face. He does have a gun and a mission: to murder his childhood hero.